British Tommy 1914–18

Martin Pegler • Illustrated by Mike Chappell

First published in Great Britain in 1996 by Osprey Publishing, Elms Court, Chapel Way, Botley, Oxford OX2 9LP, United Kingdom.
Email: info@ospreypublishing.com

ISBN 1 855325 541 1

Military Editor: Nikolai Bogdanovic
Designed by Paul Kime
Filmset in Great Britain by Keyspools Ltd.
Printed in China through World Print Ltd.

FOR A CATALOGUE OF ALL BOOKS PUBLISHED BY OSPREY MILITARY AND AVIATION PLEASE CONTACT:

The Marketing Manager, Osprey Direct UK,
PO Box 140, Wellingborough, Northants,
NN8 4ZA, United Kingdom.
Email: info@ospreydirect.co.uk

The Marketing Manager, Osprey Direct USA,
c/o Motorbooks International, PO Box 1, Osceola,
WI 54020-0001, USA.
Email: info@ospreydirectusa.com

www.ospreypublishing.com

Dedication

To ex-Privates Clarrie Jarman and Fred Dixon, both now approaching their century, Will and George Wells, Frederick Mowbray and all of the other men whose experiences have provided the basis for this book.

Acknowledgements

The Trustees of the Royal Armouries for permission to use photographs from their collection, and to Simon Dunstan, Martin Windrow, Fred Wilkinson, Richard Dunning and Tom Donovan. Also Deni for her keyboard skills, and Katie for her critical ones, and a grateful thank you to York Processing for their excellent work.

Editor's Note

Special thanks is due to Mr P. Squires and Mr G. Carefoot of the Great War Society for their expert help and collaboration on this project.

INTRODUCTION

Until the Second World War, no event in history had produced as many strong visual images and such a volume of printed material as the First World War. Poetry, letters, unit histories, autobiographies, photographs and film – all have conspired to give a popular image of the Great War, familiar to most of us. It is one of a blasted, waterlogged landscape, populated by elegant officers and grinning mud-caked Tommies, who wave jerkily at us from sepia-tinted newsreel. In the background, the ponderous military hardware of one of the most powerful industrial nations in the world rumbles along in a never-ending, silent stream. Artillery towed by puffing steam engines, aeroplanes, motorcycles, staff cars, and tanks, contrast sharply with the horse-drawn wagons, and shell-laden mules of an earlier era, and conspire to give the impression that the war had become an inexorable Titan, grinding impartially along, with humans providing no more than a supporting role.

There is a small element of truth in this vision, but the Great War was very much a conflict of infantrymen; those troglodyte, and now largely

Men of several Regular Army regiments take a meal break. They wear two different types of cap; the 1915 trench cap with neck curtain (known as the 'Gor blimey') and the 1902 service dress cap. The man second from right is dipping into the ubiquitous tin of 'Fray Bentos' corned beef. (National Army Museum)

The irrepressible Tommy: a German prisoner-of-war helps a wounded British private to the dressing station; Epehy, September 1918. (Imperial War Museum)

individuals, and this book will look in detail at how the British soldier lived, fought, and died during those traumatic war years. In addition, his weapons, uniform and equipment will be examined.

Above all, it is hoped that this book will convey some idea of what life at 'the front' was like for the ordinary infantryman.

Due to limitations of space, some areas have been ignored. The campaigns in Gallipoli, Egypt and Africa are outside the scope of this book, and the role of the regular pre-war army will be mentioned only in passing.

HISTORICAL BACKGROUND

The First World War was a watershed in British military and social history, and even now, 80 years on, its repercussions can still be felt. Women's suffrage, the rise of the Labour movement, and an increasingly vociferous anti-military stance by politicians and populace were the results of those years of terrible conflict. No town or village in the British Isles escaped their casualties, and the creative genius of a generation was wiped out, at an incalculable loss to society. The war started with all the drum thumping and banner waving that the Victorians had come to expect. Small colonial wars had been fought (and usually won) against generally ill-equipped and poorly led adversaries. Had they chosen to see it, the High Command could have had a chilling glimpse of the future during the Boer War, when the well-armed and effectively led Boer commandos repeatedly ran rings around the British Army. Such lessons as could have been learned were ignored, however. The war in 1914 was viewed in traditional terms – it would be a short sharp clash, with open warfare, and much use of cavalry (still the darlings of the General Staff) resulting in a bloody nose for the Hun, and everyone home by Christmas. In practice, it all worked out rather differently.

forgotten masses of Tommies, Fritzes, and Poilus who left little record of their lives except in frozen glimpses of time caught by a camera, or the letters and diaries salted away in family collections or museum basements. Without the ordinary soldier there could have been no war, but rarely is the infantryman looked at as an individual. Armies, corps and divisions comprised thousands of these

Germany was a formidable industrial power, politically bent on colonial expansion and it posed a direct threat to British interests world-wide. Britain was as keen to protect its interests as Germany was to expand, and the will to wage war was strong on both sides. Britain had not fought in a European war since the defeat of Napoleon in 1815, but Germany had learned much from the Franco–Prussian war of 1870. The use, or more accurately, misuse of modern technology during that conflict had left its mark upon the minds of the Prussian generals. At the outbreak of war, they had double the number of machine-guns that Britain had, as well as a prepared strategy (which fortunately was not adhered to), an understanding of the devastating power of massed artillery, and defensive capabilities of entrenched troops against attacking infantry.

The stalemate for which the war became infamous had set in by winter 1914, and lasted until spring 1918. During that time, a continuous line of trenches stretched from the Belgian coast

A group of Royal Artillerymen wearing an interesting mixture of goatskin jackets. Although warm, they were completely impractical, being smelly when wet, and becoming extremely heavy once coated in mud – the quality of which is visible on the soldiers' boots. (Imperial War Museum)

to Switzerland. Over five million Englishmen were in uniform, drawn from all the social classes, and the conflict was costing Britain £7.5 million per day. Impressive though these figures are, they do not begin to convey the true cost of the war on the people of the embattled nations, for this was total warfare: for the first time civilians far removed from the front line became legitimate and defenceless targets.

Poison gas, flamethrowers, tanks, radio communications, even the indiscriminate bombing of civilian targets all became an accepted part of warfare. By 1918 not only had the political map of Europe changed, so too had the psychology of warfare.

CHRONOLOGY

Principal battles

ENLISTMENT

It is a fact of life that men join armies for a multitude of reasons in peacetime. However, the outbreak of war in England in 1914 provoked a huge upsurge of patriotism that to modern minds is difficult to comprehend. It is therefore possible to generalise about the reasons for enlistment with perhaps more accuracy than would normally be acceptable.

Britain's professional army was small, around 247,000 men. As casualties mounted it became clear that this was insufficient to meet the needs of a European war. The Territorial army, formed in 1908 from the Volunteers and Yeomanry, provided a stopgap of trained manpower to reinforce the British Expeditionary Force but even this was rapidly proving inadequate. Gen. Kitchener's call for 100,000 volunteers was met with such an overwhelming response that the War Office could not cope. From July to November 1914, 253,195 men voluntarily enlisted in Great Britain. Never before had the War Office had to deal with such numbers of recruits. The problems

A nicely posed picture of a soldier wearing a 'PH' helmet. Its carrying bag is visible on his hip. His clothing is typical of the front line, although his casual attitude to exposing his head would seem to indicate a particularly quiet sector. Such exposure in most front lines would invite instant sniper reprisal. (Courtesy F. Wilkinson)

caused were manifold, not only logistically but socially, as classes who had hitherto only ever rubbed shoulders found themselves eating, sleeping and training together.

Why did so many young men rush to join the colours at a time when the reputation of the army was still an unsavoury one?

The answer appears to lie in three root causes: boredom, poverty and patriotism. Many veterans like Clarrie Jarman (17th Royal West Surreys) recall the excitement generated by the war, and the frustration of young men like himself stuck in futureless, poorly paid jobs: 'I was 16, and working as a sales assistant at a big hardware merchants in Woking. I earned six bob (30p) a week, and worked from 7am to 7pm six days a week. I gave most of my money to my mother. I hated being at home, and the job wasn't exciting. When the recruiting sergeants and bands came round they seemed like the most interesting thing that ever happened in Woking.' Although under age, he looked old enough to be the required 18, and enlisted with two chums in the Queens Regiment for the princely sum of 5/- (25p) a week. Tens of thousands of other young men did the same.

Poverty was a big factor. Many working-class men lived on or under the breadline, trying to support their families on minimal wages. Army doctors in 1914 noted that malnourishment was rife amongst applicants, some 44 per cent of whom could not attain the minimum 36in. chest size. For these men, the army offered a regular wage, better food, and some excitement. Fred Wood, an unskilled labourer from working-class Sheffield, commented that although his companions complained about the food, in the first six weeks of training he put on 8lb (3kg). Like most recruits he enlisted for 'The Duration' – that is, until the war ended. His army enlistment was the best thing he ever did, he comments. 'The longer it went on, the happier I was.'

Sometimes motives were mixed. Fred Dixon, who joined the Surrey Yeomanry, spoke for many in explaining why he enlisted:

'All of us were terrified that it would all be over before we got there. We all prayed that the

This relatively late war photograph shows the right-hand British soldier wearing common winter weather clothing; trench waders, a leather jerkin over the tunic with leather equipment buckled over the top, and box respirator slung over his chest. Although holding rifles, both men are wearing 1914 pattern pistol equipment. The man on the left wears a thick non-issue scarf and heavy fingerless gloves. (Courtesy F. Wilkinson)

war would continue until we had a chance to do our duty.' Therein lay the clue for the third reason for joining up. Publicity about the plight of 'poor little Belgium', stories of atrocities, and the spread of 'Hun frightfulness' aroused a genuine anger in many. Men felt that it was their duty to fight, to 'do their bit' and this sense of patriotic outrage prompted many to join up. Fred Wood recalled his feelings at the time:

'People then were very naive ... we believed the newspaper reports, and one evening my chum Ginger said, "We shouldn't let them get away with it." We all agreed, so four of us went to the recruiting office and signed up. I was the only one who came back alive in 1918, though.'

The procedure for enlisting was straightforward enough. Local recruitment centres were set up in

A Lewis-gun post in an immaculate trench: whilst the left-hand man peers through a box-periscope, his companion poses in a British warm greatcoat and trench waders. The Lewis gun sits at readiness, with boxed ammunition in the left foreground. The state of this trench is in marked contrast to that of the next illustration. (Courtesy F. Wilkinson)

Territorial army drill halls or local town halls. Volunteers were given a basic medical examination, and if they passed swore an oath of allegiance, accepted the King's shilling, and returned home to await their call-up. The minimum age was 18, but recruiting officers turned a blind eye to many well-built youths, as in the case of 15-year-old George Dawson, a railway engine cleaner, who enlisted in the 1st Battalion Lincolnshire Regiment and was serving in France at the age of 16. However, with so many enlisting, recruiting officers could afford to be rather more choosy in 1914 than later in the war.

If there was an overwhelming surge of patriotism amongst many men, there was an equal level of disinterest amongst others. In many instances this was due to a lack of belief that the war would last for more than a matter of weeks, but there was a strong core of pacifists who did not believe in war as a means of solving political disputes. Many were imprisoned for their beliefs, but others like George Wells opted to join the RAMC as an orderly.

'I believed then, as I still do, that there was no possible justification for killing, but I had no objection to saving lives. Many of my Quaker friends suffered because of public abuse, but I escaped all that because of being in uniform.'

Older men with settled careers and families were more reluctant to join up. They were not so swayed by lurid tales of German atrocities, and far less inclined to leave secure jobs for glory or excitement.

Many men were in jobs deemed vital for the war effort, and were refused permission to enlist. This was not a happy state of affairs for those who saw the army as a means of escape from a tedious job, and large numbers of men joined under assumed names to escape detection by irate bosses who could ill afford to lose skilled labour. Tom Setchell was a machinist making parts for engines. After two applications to his manager for permission to enlist were refused, he joined up under a false name and never went back to his old profession. He said that 'never once did I regret the choice. I ended up in the Engineers, and became a professional soldier after the war.'

By July 1915 the National Registration Act had recorded all men aged between 18 and 41, and in October of the same year the Derby Scheme created a system of short-term enlistment, with men then being placed on reserve until called up. Single men who were fit enough to serve were becoming a rare commodity by the end of 1915, so in January 1916 conscription was introduced. This meant all single men up to age 41 could be conscripted, and this was then extended to all married men later in the year. So scarce was manpower by 1918 that the age for service was increased to 51. Up until February 1916, 2,631,000 men had volunteered. Conscription increased the number by another 2,340,000.

By whatever means the government ensured that a man joined the army, there was no doubt that the world the men entered was unlike anything they had ever experienced before.

TRAINING

Recruitment

Enlisting was a relatively straightforward process providing one had plenty of patience. Huge crowds surrounded the temporary recruitment offices, with the police attempting to keep some semblance of order. For the new recruit, the process of taking the King's shilling was as much a matter of having patience as well as a good constitution and his own teeth. Once inside, a form of attestation was filled out: the biggest problem for many was the age factor (18 being the minimum). Many hopeful 16-year-olds were eyed speculatively by a regular sergeant and told, 'Hop it, and come back tomorrow when you're 18', followed by a conspiratorial wink.

The medical examination was not detailed. A doctor would check for obvious defects in eyesight, teeth and chest. TB was still endemic amongst working-class men and any sufferers would be summarily rejected. Those considered sound of mind and body were told to return home, where they would be given instructions in due course. Many who were rejected simply went to other recruiting stations where standards were known to be lower. Fred Wood, at 5ft 6in. and with a 32in. chest, was turned away with the suggestion he 'got a bit bigger'. He therefore went to another area in his native Sheffield and was accepted without question.

Joining instructions for training battalions arrived at varying times. Some men received them within a week, others began to think the army didn't want them at all. Most were told to report to their local training depot. Clarrie Jarman was marched straight out of the recruitment hall to Stoughton barracks, home of the Queen's Regiment. The following day all the new recruits were sent by train to Purfleet in Essex, where they

A recently constructed trench on the Somme, typical of the terrain that front-line soldiers fought and died in: this example houses a Vickers machine-gun crew, the tripod and pile of empty cartridges being visible mid-centre of the photograph. A knocked-out Mk 1 female tank is slumped in the background. (Tank Museum, Bovington)

lived in tents from August 1914 to April 1915.

Training was designed not so much to teach the men the art of war as to toughen them. Drill, bayonet fighting, musketry and French digging were all taught. For men who were urban dwellers, the constant physical exercise was tough. Pvt. Jarman recalled a typical training exercise as follows:

'We marched from Colchester to Ipswich, 18 miles, where we stayed one night, then in five days we covered 150 miles over the Suffolk moors, living rough. We arrived back at Ipswich at 10pm. We were then roused at 11pm and made to march all night back to Colchester.'

A German entanglement on the Hindenberg Line: such dense masses of barbed wire could be up to 100 yards wide. Artillery bombardment served only to pile the wire into impenetrable thickets, and it was only the advent of the tank that eventually defeated it. Some success was had with Bangalor torpedoes, metal tubes packed with explosive, but they were both difficult and dangerous to use. (Courtesy F. Wilkinson)

Logistics

The organisation of food, clothing and billeting for the new volunteers was a massive undertaking, which took some time to organise. All over the country, Kitchener's new recruits were despatched to temporary billets, often miles from their training areas, and into the hands of redoubtable landladies, some of whom were less than pleased to have soldiers foisted upon them. There were wildly varying conditions dependent on area. Soldiers who joined locally raised units could find themselves treated as heroes by the populace, with free beer in the local pub and landladies who took to them as if they were their own sons. Fred Wood, by then in a Northern Cyclist Battalion, found the opposite.

'We seemed to be nobody's children. We had no uniforms, so wore a khaki armband, and had to buy our own food. Pay was very irregular, and we had to walk four miles to be on parade at 6am. We got old Metfords [rifles] in February 1915, then spent all our time doing bayonet charges.'

With army pay of 5/- (25p), rations allowance of 14s 7d (73p) and a retainer from their old firms, usually of half their weekly wage, some recruits had never been so well off. If their finances were improved, their humour was not by

army discipline and the monotonous training exercises devised before the Boer War, and rigidly adhered to as late as 1917. The concept of the machine-gun was ignored, and soldiers were instructed in the art of marching in open formation towards 'the enemy' with the sole intention of 'getting to grips with the bayonet'. Fred Dixon wryly commented that 'most instructors were elderly regulars, who never heard a shot in anger. They bullied us, threatened us, but taught us nothing that was of any use in France. You learned that when you got there, if you lived long enough.' Much training consisted of endless drilling, intended to turn a man into an order-obeying machine. The more intelligent soldiers found this offensive, and some officers felt it robbed men of their initiative. This was particularly the case in the huge holding and drafting camps which sprang up around the coastal regions of France. As the demand for men increased, so did the need to speed up the passage of new recruits to the front. Many of these depots became notorious for the bullying that went on, and few men had a good word to say for them.

When not drilling, fatigues were the order of the day. Men had little spare time or energy for relaxation whilst training, and bitterly resented the dozens of sometimes pointless tasks devised for them by NCOs. Aside from guard and cookhouse duties, these could include polishing every conceivable article of military hardware, such as hobnails on boots, horse shoes, mess tins and bayonet blades. Some men accepted this as part of an inevitable process; others, particularly the better educated middle-class volunteers, considered it demeaning and unnecessary. The length of time spent training varied from unit to unit. Clarrie Jarman's unit trained from August 1914 to November 1915, although his observation on this was that they were taught nothing of any great relevance about trench warfare.

Until the early months of 1917 training followed a set pattern. Men were taught to drill, march and drill some more. Pvt. Jarman, then a keen athlete, quite enjoyed the physical demands of training, but was sceptical of its practical value:

'We went on route marches, cross-country runs and were drilled like guardsmen. Sometimes we would have bayonet practice against a straw dummy and two or three times we went to the ranges, but that was as close to fighting training as we got. We had to learn that at the front.'

Indeed combat training was conspicuously lacking from the official manual, written as it was in the days of open warfare. Men were instructed never to lie down and seek cover when advancing, but to walk steadily towards the enemy. Even pausing to fire was frowned upon, official thinking being that given the slightest excuse men would fling their weapons away and retreat, traits which the men of the Great War rarely exhibited. The appalling casualties inflicted brought about a gradual change in thinking by the close of the Somme campaign. It had become clear to even the most wooden-headed commanders that the war could not be sustained if losses continued at the rate they were. One estimate suggested that by mid-1918 16-year-old boys would have to be conscripted merely to continue the war effort at its current level. The entry of the United States proved this to be a pessimistic forecast: nevertheless, there was no doubt that lives could no longer be squandered in such a cavalier fashion. Ironically, it was the change in tactical emphasis on the part of the German army that

had brought into question the relevance of the existing tactical doctrine.

Germany had evolved a system of attack using shock troops (Sturmtruppen), well-armed but lightly equipped units which would spearhead an assault, striking at strongpoints, machine-gun positions and observation posts, robbing the enemy command of its defensive capability then moving on to let infantry units clear up. Although the Allies never entirely adopted the same system, a much more flexible approach to infantry assault had become evident by 1917. Fred Mowbray, who enlisted in 1917, recounted that:

'We were taught things like advancing in short rushes and giving covering fire. As a Lewis gunner, I was told how to target pillboxes to make

Fatigues were an integral part of every soldier's life. Men on 'rest' frequently had to make trips to the front line carrying all manner of trench stores. These men carry screw-pickets and wire netting. The exhaustion on the face of the front soldier is evident. Note no equipment or side arms are worn, only the gas mask in its haversack. (Courtesy Trustees of Royal Armouries)

the Germans keep their heads down whilst the infantry went in with grenades. It all seemed very real and frightening. Not like I thought soldiering was going to be.'

The tactical doctrines of pre-1914 had to change, in the same way that the technology of the war changed. It is tragic that so many died before the lessons were learned.

UNIFORM AND EQUIPMENT

For the front-line soldier, the issue uniform did not change to any great extent during the war

A remarkably cheery group of men on fatigues, warmly clad in an assortment of jerkins, waders, scarves and gloves: the state of the 'road' on which they stand gives some idea of conditions that had to be endured in autumn and winter. (Imperial War Museum)

years. The Kitchener recruits faced an acute shortage of almost everything, and were initially issued with blue serge uniforms until supplies of khaki arrived. Once it did, the soldier could expect to live, sleep, fight and die in it. The service dress comprised a hip-length four-pocket jacket, with a collar that buttoned up to the neck. The trousers had provision for braces on the outside and vertical slash pockets in the side seams, and were of the same rough woollen serge cloth as the tunic. Worn with the issue long drawers, long-sleeved vest and heavy flannel shirt the wearer became unbearably hot in summer, as Pvt. Jarman recalled.

'In summer on long route marches, the boys would be running with perspiration, and some of the new recruits, who weren't as fit as us, fainted from the heat. Even in shirtsleeve order it was hot. We wore the same uniform summer or winter.' An unofficial but popular summer modification to the trousers was to cut the legs off to make shorts.

In addition, B5 ammunition boots with

hobnailed soles were standard issue at the start of the war. They were made from reversed hide (undyed), had steel plates on the toes and heels, and were heavily greased. Woollen puttees were wound about the lower legs. Fred Wood was reduced to helpless laughter by the attempts of his fellows to tie the puttees neatly:

'Some chaps had them tied from ankle to knees, others wound them round and round their calves like bandages. We were saved by an older man who had served in the Boer War, who showed us the trick. They were awful things.' In subsequent trench warfare, it was found that tightly wound puttees restricted the blood flow to the feet to such an extent that trench foot and even gangrene could occur in the constant wet and muddy conditions.

Headgear was a simple soft peaked cap, which soon had its wire support removed to give it a battered look. Later the 'Gor blimey' (a soft cap with ear flaps) was issued, to be replaced by a soft cap without flaps. This new trench cap had a more military appearance than the 'Gor blimey' and could be rolled or folded and put away when the shrapnel helmet was worn. The trench cap was standard issue from 1917 onwards. However many soldiers retained their 'Gor blimey' caps where possible for use in winter weather.

There were several types of personal equipment in use at this time. Regular and territorial battalions were issued the 1908 pattern web equipment. New army units (those raised under

The upper rifle is a Mk I Lee-Metford; the lower one is a Mk I Short Magazine Lee-Enfield. The Metford was adopted in 1888, but was already being phased out by 1903 in favour of the new improved SMLE. However, a crtical shortage of weapons ensured that new recruits were often issued with Metfords, or even obsolete or foreign rifles until supplies of SMLEs became available. The distinctive shortness of the SMLE was to permit its easy carriage on a cavalry saddle. The standard SMLE at the outbreak of the war was the Mk III.
(Courtesy Trustees of Royal Armouries)

the Kitchener volunteer system) were usually issued the 1914 pattern leather equipment. Will Wells, who arrived in France with the 'Manchesters' early in 1916, noted that:

'We were told to hand in our old leather equipment, and were given salvaged sets of webbing. Mine was stiff with dried blood, and I swapped it for a decent set as soon as I could.'

1908 pattern equipment comprised a pack and a haversack, a set of ammunition pouches holding 150 .303in. rounds of ammunition, an entrenching tool, a water bottle and a mess tin. The pack and haversack might contain spare socks, shirt, underwear, a greatcoat, blanket, emergency rations and washing and shaving kit. A popular army joke featured a small boy asking his father, 'What are soldiers for?' 'To hang things on' was the reply. The latest addition to His Majesty's Army found it too true to be funny. A full set of equipment could weigh in excess of 70lb (32kg), about the same as a medieval suit of armour.

The most instantly recognisable symbol of the British Tommy was, of course, the steel helmet.

13

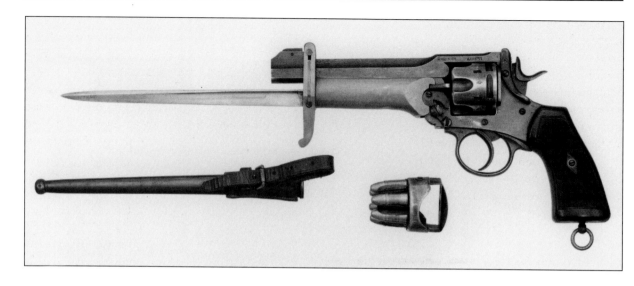

A Mk VI Webley revolver, with the curious Pritchard-Greener trench bayonet. The Webley was a sound design, well-liked by soldiers, which is more than could be said for the bayonet. It was a good idea in theory, but failed to catch on in practice. Also shown is a Prideaux speed loading device. It held six .455in. cartridges in spring clips, enabling the chambers to be refilled almost instantly. (Courtesy Trustees of Royal Armouries)

These were issued on a trial basis late in 1915, and were officially referred to as 'shrapnel helmets'. So effective were they in preventing fatal head wounds (a reduction of 80 per cent was calculated) that full-scale production was authorised by the government, and by the end of the war over 7.5 million had been manufactured. Initially, many soldiers found them irritating:

'I had worn a soft hat since the start [of the war] and the steel helmet felt like a lump of lead on my head. I hated it until a lump of shrapnel knocked me senseless at Cambrai. It saved my life, and I regarded it with some fondness afterwards.' (J. Dalton, Tank Corps.) The helmet was designed so that the chinstrap retaining rivets would shear in the event of the helmet being blown off: this would avoid garroting the wearer or breaking his neck. Experienced soldiers in action wore the helmet tilted slightly forward for maximum protection.

Another vital piece of headgear was that potent symbol of the war, the anti-gas mask. Early lachrymatory and sternutatory gases had the same effect as tear gas, although they rarely proved

fatal. The first masks were simply cotton wool pads soaked in neutralising chemicals, or urine if no chemical was available. These were replaced by the 'P' and 'PH' helmet (so called because the fabric of the helmet was impregnated with a chemical solution, Phenate Hexamine). The wearer breathed in through the nose, drawing air through the material of the hood and out through the mouthpiece, which was a simple non-return valve.

In late 1916 the box respirator was introduced. This was a rubberised mask with a long tube attached to a filtration unit. Jim Marshall had reason to be grateful for his. Whilst carrying his Vickers into position at Arras, his team came under sudden bombardment.

'Our sergeant noticed that some shells were not exploding, and called, "Gas, gas!" We dropped everything and pulled our masks on, but not before we had taken a whiff of it. I was coughing something terrible, but daren't take the mask off. We had to lug the guns into position, mount them and stand at readiness all with the masks on. It was a couple of hours later that an officer came up and asked why we still had our masks on, as the all clear had been sounded ages before. Our sergeant felt a right fool, but we reckoned better safe than sorry. We was all frightened of gas.' Once an effective means of combating gas had been introduced its use as a practical weapon diminished, but it still exacted a steady toll of casualties throughout the war.

As with any army on a period of long active service, issue clothing was modified, adapted or discarded according to need and conditions. It became clear that the service clothing was deficient in some respects. Greatcoats were not waterproof, and once weighted down with rain and mud soon became unwearable. Boots and puttees were impractical in sodden trenches, and the tunic was not warm enough in winter. Men often added their own clothing sent out from home, or purchased locally, and most wore home-made sweaters, scarves and socks. The problem of supplying warm clothing that did not hamper movement was addressed by the War Office, and in 1915 goatskin jerkins were issued. Pvt. Dalton, initially sent to Flanders with the Royal Marines, noted that although 'they were quite warm, they stank to high heaven when they were wet, and soon became clogged with mud'. In late 1916, a sleeveless leather jerkin with a blanket lining was issued. This proved both comfortable and durable, and remained in service for numerous years afterwards. For wet weather there was a rubberised cape (introduced 1917), with a collar and a button-up front. Although hot to wear, it was genuinely waterproof, and could also be used as a groundsheet, or attached to another to form a shelter. Prior to this soldiers used a rectangular groundsheet, which was draped over the shoulders.

Protection for the legs was more difficult. Wrapping empty sandbags around calves and thighs gave additional warmth and to a certain extent protected against the mud. Thigh-length waders became an important part of trench clothing. These were issued as fixed stores, and would be inherited by each battalion upon taking over a new trench. They were only effective up to a point, as Harry Wood experienced.

'On our way we passed a man stuck to his waist in a drainage sump. We gathered round and got some trench timbers under his arms to give him support. We pulled him out eventually but he left behind his waders, boots and trousers. He was so exhausted he had to be stretchered to an aid post.' There was less latitude with headgear, particularly in view of the necessity of wearing a steel helmet for protection. In winter, a cap comforter was often worn underneath. This was a simple woollen tube which doubled as a hat or scarf. Soft caps were invariably worn out of the line.

Many tests were carried out with bulletproof waistcoats, and a number of types were privately purchased. Examples such as Dayfield, BEF, Wilkinson and Pullman were a few of those available. In 1917 the EOB (Experimental Ordnance Board) was issued officially on a limited basis. Like most of its type it was heavy at 9.5lb (4.3kg) and hot to wear, but it could stop a service

A major logistical problem was ensuring that hot food and water were delivered to front-line units, many of whom were unable to light fires or obtain unpolluted water. This soldier carries an insulated food container (these were filled with hot water once the contents has been sealed in), in addition to his full equipment. Taking such a load through darkened, muddy trenches was a considerable physical effort. (Courtesy F. Wilkinson)

.455 pistol bullet, or a rifle round providing it was not travelling at more than 1,000 fps, about one third of its initial velocity.

On the whole, British clothing was solidly made and there were few shortages, which, considering the number of men to be clothed, is quite remarkable. Some of the logistical statistics are quite mind numbing. For example 45,351,488 pairs of boots and 137,224,141 pairs of socks were supplied in four years! It is worth noting that few soldiers were ever seen wearing items of pilfered German clothing, whereas by 1917, British boots, jerkins and groundsheets had become prized booty amongst German troops.

WEAPONS

The rifle

The outbreak of war saw the British Army equipped with the Short Magazine Lee-Enfield (SMLE), but soon the old Long Lee Enfield and a variety of other weapons were pressed into service.

With the introduction of the SMLE in 1903 Britain became the first major power to abandon the idea of issuing carbines to cavalry units and rifles to infantry. The SMLE was issued to both. It was shorter and lighter than any other current service rifle of the time and usefully, as it turned out, was easier to wield than the Mauser in the close confines of a trench.

It took some skill to master, and most young recruits developed a healthy respect for the recoil, as Fred Dixon remembered:

'We were taken to the ranges in Colchester and issued with 25 rounds of .303 [ammunition]. The instructor went through the safety routine, then told us to fire 10 rounds aimed. I didn't hold the butt tight enough into my shoulder, and when I pulled the trigger I was sure I'd broken my collar bone. Firing the rest was agony, and I was black and blue for a week after.'

Many soldiers were shipped to France having barely mastered the art of shooting, and the skill at arms of the pre-war Regular Army had

A carrying party working their way through a trench. The front two men carry insulated food containers. Note that in the background are stacked four signal rockets, and also the carefully wrapped rifle of the man second from the right. Sandbags, socks or old uniform were employed to keep the mechanism and the barrel mud-free. All the men have sandbag covers over their shrapnel helmets.
(Courtesy Trustees of Royal Armouries)

vanished by 1916. For trench fighting, the rifle was really not the most practical weapon, particularly when 17 inches of bayonet was attached to it. It was, however, extremely powerful, the bullet being capable of penetrating 18in. (457mm) of oak, 36in. (914mm) of earth-packed sandbags, as well as a double thickness of housebricks at 200 yards (185m). In skilled hands, hits at 1,000 yards (925m) were quite feasible, the bullet having an extreme aimed range of over double that distance.

Pistols, hand grenades and trench clubs

For close combat work, infantrymen often obtained pistols (captured German Lugers were a great favourite), particularly when patrols or trench raiding were called for. Although not officially issued to infantrymen, revolvers were carried by specialists, such as machine-gunners, despatch riders, tank crew and Royal Engineers. The three most commonly issued types were all in service .455in. calibre, and comprised the Mk V or VI Webley, Colt New Service, and Smith & Wesson Hand Ejector. All were difficult to shoot well without considerable practice, although the heavy bullets were effective. Perhaps the skill required to master the rifle and pistol were one of the reasons for the popularity of the hand grenade, more of which were issued than any other form of weapon. Over 61 million were produced, of which the most effective type was the No. 5, commonly known as the 'Mills' bomb. It had a simple spring-actuated fuse mechanism, and could be thrown quite accurately to about 30 yards. It had a tendency to break into irregular fragments on detonation, due to the offset (as opposed to central) position of the explosive. The

Mills bomb was extremely effective and survived long into the post Second World War era. Corporal James Allsop testified to its efficiency in a raid in June 1916:

'We had to get prisoners, so we had a big "do" set up. I was one of the mopping up party, to make sure the Jerries didn't come out of their dugouts behind us. Well, we put up a barricade in the [German] trench and as our chaps headed back with prisoners, Jerry came at us. We couldn't hold them back, and they brought a Maxim up, so I lobbed a bomb and ducked behind the traverse. When the smoke cleared there were six Jerries on the ground. The rest hid, they wouldn't argue with a Mills.'

Often criticised for their failure to provide cooked food on demand, company cooks had an unenviable task. Working in the open with primitive equipment and inadequate supplies of fuel they were expected to provide meals for hundreds of men, at any time of day or night. Here, cooks tend 'Dixies', oval-shaped camp kettles.
(Courtesy F. Wilkinson)

Home-made and issue trench clubs were also handy weapons in a fight, and came in a variety of shapes and sizes.

Entrenching tool handles studded with nails, cut-down machine-gun barrels and sprung steel coshes all made an appearance. Issue clubs usually comprised a length of stout wood with a rough cast-iron head, or steel cap. All were crude, but effective enough, as were the trench knives used. Sheath knives, cut-down bayonets and a number of proprietary knives such as the Robbins punch dagger and bizarre Pritchard revolver bayonet were all carried, although little evidence exists of their use in action. As one wit dryly remarked of the bayonet; 'it has no place in warfare except as a candleholder, in which capacity it excels.'

Officers had abandoned their swords after 1914, but not so the cavalry, who were issued with the pattern 1908 sword. Designed for thrusting, its clean lines and slim blade made it an effective weapon. Failed attempts to use cavalry against barbed wire and machine-guns did not sway the High Command from their belief that the mounted service would effect a dashing breakthrough. Most ended the war as dismounted infantrymen, armed with the universal SMLE.

Machine-guns

At platoon and battalion level, machine-guns had begun to dominate tactics by 1915. Most were based on the Maxim design, and although reliable, they were costly to manufacture, complex to operate (it took 10 intensive weeks to train a Vickers gunner) and very cumbersome. A loaded Vickers weighed about 100lb (45kg) and consumed huge quantities of ammunition. In a long-range barrage, a single gun could easily fire 100,000 rounds, with some companies recording nearly a million fired rounds over a 24-hour period. Although it was extremely efficient, it was clear from early in the war that a lighter automatic weapon was needed, and this came in the form of the American-designed Lewis gun.

The Lewis was the first effective light machine-gun issued, although 'light' was a relative term, as a loaded one weighed an impressive 29lb (13.1kg). With its 550 rpm cyclic rate it gave a squad of infantry the equivalent firepower of a section. Its 47-round drum magazine produced a distinctive football rattle clatter when the weapon was fired, and although it was prone to a bewildering number of stoppages (one manual lists 33) it was well liked. Fred Mowbray, a private in the King's Royal Rifle Corps, was a Lewis gunner, and liked

its solid build quality as well as the effectiveness of its firepower. His section, held up by a pillbox during the advance of 1918, called him forward to deal with the defenders. He emptied two drums through the firing slit and rushed the box. Although he had knocked out the Maxim crew inside, a second gun hidden behind the pillbox caught him with a sweeping burst. Hit across the arms and stomach by six bullets, the impact lifted him off his feet, flinging him and his gun into a shell crater. With bullets through his left hand and right elbow, his war, but not his life, was over. He was still alive because the solid steel receiver and breech assembly of the Lewis absorbed the impact of the other rounds. He had hated the weight of the Lewis, but commented wryly that 'the old Lewis gave me as much protection as a suit of armour. Mind you, it was nearly as heavy.'

Other weapons

The trenches were a breeding ground for weapons, many of them bordering on the bizarre. Some were designed as a response to a specific need, whilst others appear to have resulted from mental aberrations on the part of the inventor. Some, like the West bomb-thrower, were

One of the great civilising influences on the British soldier serving in France or Flanders was the willingness of local people to provide food in a homely atmosphere – usually for a very modest outlay. Here an elderly French woman cooks whilst her husband reads. Three British soldiers appear to await the culinary delight with great interest. (Courtesy Trustees of Royal Armouries)

theoretically quite sound. It was no more than a small steel-framed variant of a medieval trebuchet, relying on several very strong coil springs to provide power, and fling a hand grenade several hundred yards. However, the springs proved so strong that several operators were injured when the machine fired itself prematurely. Others flung live grenades into the parapet of their own trenches.

The problem of grenade launching was soon solved by either attaching a short rod to a Mills bomb, or fitting a steel discharger cup to the muzzle of an SMLE, both of which would safely launch a grenade.

The service rifle was often the means by which less than practical inventions were introduced to the luckless infantryman. Two ideas that were issued in some quantity offered solutions to the problem of wire cutting. One comprised a spring-loaded pair of jaws that required the rifle

to be used as a lever, forcing the cutting edges together and (theoretically) severing the wire. This required the hapless soldier to stand upright, unwise when in full view of the enemy. The other was a forked bar that clamped onto the rifle's muzzle, which was then pushed over the wire strand, and the trigger pulled. The bullet then cut the wire. As many belts of wire were yards deep, the amount of ammunition one man would have to expend is best left to the imagination.

Other weapons were more practical. Trench mortars, invaluable for their almost vertical trajectory, were an area in which Britain lagged behind Germany. The first British pattern fired a 60lb (27.2kg) spherical cast-iron bomb, nicknamed the 'Toffee Apple', attached to a steel shaft. On firing, the shaft often snapped, leaving the eventual destination of the bomb uncertain, and a direct hit improbable. However, from this early design of projector emerged the highly successful Stokes mortar (illustrated in colour plate K), which in turn was the model upon which the

majority of modern mortar designs are based.

Trench warfare also showed up the deficiencies in service weapons. A rifle and bayonet were too cumbersome for trench fighting, but curiously, Britain made no attempt to produce a practical semi-automatic rifle or submachine-gun, unlike Germany and France. The US army introduced the eminently practical Model 1897 Winchester pump-action shotgun decried by the War Ministry as 'un-military'. Semi-automatic pistols did make a significant appearance, however, as mud often clogged service revolvers, an occurrence to which semi-autos were relatively impervious. In addition, they were quicker to reload, had a greater cartridge capacity, and found favour with both officers and other ranks. Jim Marshall had a rare Webley .455in. semi-automatic. 'I got it from an Aussie, who had got it from a pilot. It was a lovely gun, and during the big retreat in 1918 I used it in anger several times. I modified my holster to carry it, and nobody said I couldn't. The only trouble was ammunition, as it took special .45in. cartridges. It was very powerful, and quite accurate. I shot a Jerry machine-gunner, and one of my section gave me his helmet. The bullet had gone clean through, and I measured the distance afterwards at 45 yards.'

Many of the lessons learned about infantry weapons were forgotten afterwards. When Will Wells joined the Home Guard in 1940 he was bemused to be issued with a 1916 dated SMLE. 'I asked if we had any tommy guns and was told, "We didn't need them in the last war and won't in this one".'

ACTIVE SERVICE

Trench life

Few men had any real concept of the realities of life 'at the front'. For most recruits, their first taste of the war was an audible one, as Clarrie Jarman recalled:

'We arrived at Amiens by train, and could hear a rumble in the distance, which was the artillery. We marched to Dornancourt and went into the line for the first time. The bullets whizzed and cracked, and made us duck. The shells whined overhead, but we learned quickly when to take cover and when not to.' The trenches varied greatly in construction and comfort. In Belgium, the high water table prevented deep trenches being dug, so breastworks of sandbags with wooden retaining supports were constructed. In France the chalky soil lent itself well to deep trenches, with high parapets built up with sandbags giving some cover against sniping. Deep dugouts gave protection to HQs and resting soldiers, and during heavy bombardments. However, for most a 'funk hole' scraped into the facing wall of the trench, and lined with rubber capes, was the best that could be expected. It was not the policy of the general staff to encourage

An orders group, Bailleul, 16 April 1918: officers of a battalion of the Middlesex Regiment are being briefed by an officer of the Scottish Rifles. Runners wait expectantly in the rear. (Imperial War Museum)

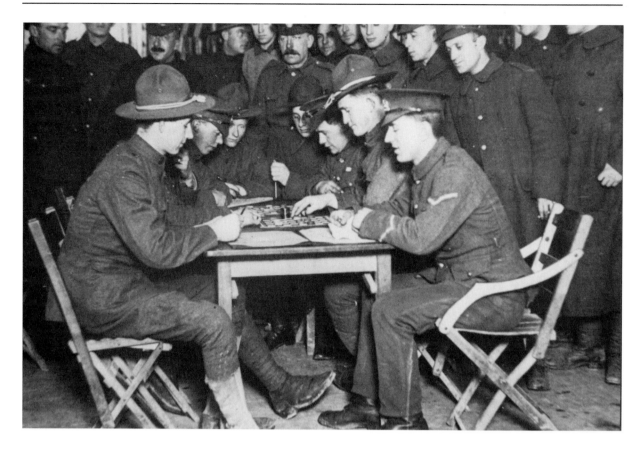

British troops play Americans at chequers, probably for the benefit of the camera. Pontoon, crown and anchor or poker were more likely to be played, with heavy betting on the outcome. Few British soldiers enjoyed betting against their allies. Australians, Canadians and Americans were all payed more and heavy losses could result in feelings running high. (Courtesy Trustees of Royal Armouries)

British troops to make themselves too comfortable, as it was felt that it discouraged 'the offensive spirit'. The Germans had no such qualms, and built concrete-lined dugouts as deep as 60ft (18m) beneath the ground – impervious to the heaviest shelling. Trench routine was physically demanding. 'Stand to' was at dawn, where all troops would man the trench in expectation of an enemy attack. Wet weather was universally hated. In Flanders, the poor drainage often forced both sides to abandon their trenches for higher ground, as water levels rose to waist height. A tacit truce was usually observed. The chalk of the Somme clung in 10lb balls to men's feet and exhausted even the fittest of men. Such conditions meant that a 500 yard (460m) journey could take several hours. If the line was being shelled, or under sniper fire, then those manning the trenches were effectively trapped until nightfall. Winter conditions reduced the line to a series of sludge-filled ditches, from which there was no escape, save leave or a wound. But if winter was grim, it was more than compensated for by spring and summer. The shell-churned soil became ablaze with poppies, cornflowers and a host of other species. Larks, unaccountably still resident, would hover, trilling in the sky. Few soldiers forgot the beauty that sprang up amidst the desolation, even in the face of battle. Some never had the chance to adapt to trench life. Curiosity was a killer, and any who risked a look over the parapet seldom lived to repeat the experience. 16-year-old Pvt. George Dawson was shot in the head on his first day in the trenches, dying shortly afterwards. Until 1915 German snipers, who had learned their trade hunting in the vast German forests, dominated the trenches, but by 1916 Britain was producing well-trained men more than capable of controlling no man's land.

Occupation of the trenches depended upon conditions. A usual tour of duty was four to seven days in the line, the same in reserve and a week at rest. At Passchendaele in 1917, torrential rain and broken drainage ditches turned the ground into a swamp and 24 hours was the maximum men could stand such exposure. After major battles, particularly hard-hit units would be placed in quiet sectors, where unofficial 'live and let live' policies ensured that front-line service was not too arduous. That being so, average casualties in 'quiet' sectors would be 40 per month. There was no such thing as a safe place at the front, as Jim Marshall of the Machine-gun Corps had learned.

'We had just come out of the line, and were heading back to our billets when Jerry dropped a couple of shells in front of us. We didn't take any notice, they were always doing it, when there was an almighty roar and flash. Next thing I was lying in the road yards away. I had my tunic ripped off and the tripod [for the Vickers gun] vanished. I was completely deaf, but not hurt much. They never found two of my chums and the other died

An Australian company on the march: the photo well illustrates the weight of equipment carried. Several men carry two haversacks (one containing the small box respirator) as well as blankets, rolled greatcoats, mess tin, and other paraphernalia. An average load would be 60–70lb. (Courtesy Trustees of Royal Armouries)

at the aid post.'

As many soldiers saw it, trench life was '90 per cent routine and 10 per cent terror'. The hardest thing to endure was shellfire. There were no means of retaliation for the ordinary infantryman, who had no option but to seek the deepest shelter possible and endure it. The older men held up better under fire than the young ones, whom they would try to encourage. Jim Wooley of the West Yorkshire Regiment recalled a four-hour bombardment in a dugout full of shell fumes, with dirt falling from the creaking roof timbers.

'We had a new lad, who'd not been with us long. After a bit he started sobbing, and one of our chaps who had a young son moved next to him and put his arms round him. After a bit the lad began to recover. Things like that

An unusual photograph of a rifle-grenade pit: the SMLE rifle has a Hales grenade inserted into the barrel (the adjustable bipod permitted the weapon to be fired at the required angle). Few grenade-launching rifles were used for any other purpose, as firing rodded-grenades soon ruined barrels. The practical effect of such grenades was minimal, but the effect on morale was more tangible. (Private collection)

often happened.'

Trench mortars were also a feared hazard, but could be beaten. In trenches known to be targeted, a lookout would watch for the tell-tale black speck of a mortar bomb rising from the German lines. He would then blow a whistle to alert men, and if he was experienced enough shout 'Left!' or 'Right!' to indicate the direction they should run to escape the blast. The explosive effect from the bigger mortars was devastating, and those caught in the proximity stood no chance. Fred Wood was one of a working party called to find survivors after such a detonation. Ten men were missing, but only sufficient remains were found to fill two sandbags. If the site of the mortars could be pinpointed, calls were placed to the artillery for emergency retaliation, which invariably raised a cheer from the British lines. In extreme cases, the artillery could also be called upon to deal with a persistent sniper.

For much of the time, trench life was a regime of monotonous routine with dangerous overtones. The stress of living under the constant threat of sudden death or wounding affected men in different ways. Some simply couldn't take the strain and went absent, risking a capital sentence from a court-martial.

Others found ways of disabling themselves, the most common being using a rifle to shoot themselves through the hand or foot. Some would deliberately expose an arm or shoulder above the trench to encourage a sniper's shot. Such self-inflicted wounds, if discovered, were severely dealt with by the army. The soldiers themselves took a less judgmental view. Fred Wood, a sergeant by then, spoke for many.

A Lewis-gun section takes cover during the advance of 1918. The men are in fighting order and have rolled groundsheets inside their haversacks. The man nearest the camera also has a full ration bag. To the left are a pair of webbing panniers for carrying Lewis gun drums.
(National Army Museum)

'By 1918 those of us who had survived were sick to death of the war. We reckoned we'd done our bit, and it was up to the shirkers who'd avoided the war to have a go. I was very fatalistic by then. I didn't think I could survive, and wondered how I had managed up till then. When a chum of mine, who'd been out since 1915, reported to the MO with a bullet through the hand we knew it hadn't been an accident. But we didn't blame him at all. Many times I wished I'd had the courage to do the same.'

FOOD

Predictably, the soldier's main preoccupation was for his stomach. The official rations for British soldiers in the line would have raised a cheer had they always been issued – 1½lb fresh meat or 1lb salt meat, 1lb biscuit or flour. 4oz bacon, 3oz cheese, ½lb tea, 4oz jam, 3oz sugar, 2oz dried or 8oz fresh vegetable, 2oz tobacco and ½ a gill of rum per day. Front-line troops were frequently hungry, as rations failed to reach them through shelling or improper allocations. Pvt. Jarman

noted that 'our main food in the line was bully stew. We shared one loaf between four men. Sometimes a ration of cheese or butter would arrive, usually when we had no bread. Tins of biscuits were always there to eat. They were like dog biscuits.'

The ubiquitous hard tack biscuit was the colour and consistency of concrete, 3½ x 4in. (90 x 100mm) and could crack teeth if bitten into. When pulverised by a rifle butt and mixed with bully beef, it could be fried, or soaked overnight and mixed with currants and dried fruit and boiled into a duff. In cold weather, when no charcoal was available, it also burned satisfactorily. Some soldiers even believed that attached to an entrenching tool handle, it would make a fearsome club.

Fred Wood's opinion of the rations is largely unprintable. 'After "stand-to" we'd cook breakfast. This was usually some old bacon with bits of sandbag stuck to it, fried up in a Dixie. The only things we ever had plenty of to eat was bully, biscuits and plum and apple jam. Out of the line we spent all our money on food. If the carrying party could get through the shells, we'd have hot stew for lunch. If not it was bloody bully stew again. Sometimes we'd have Maconochie [a brand

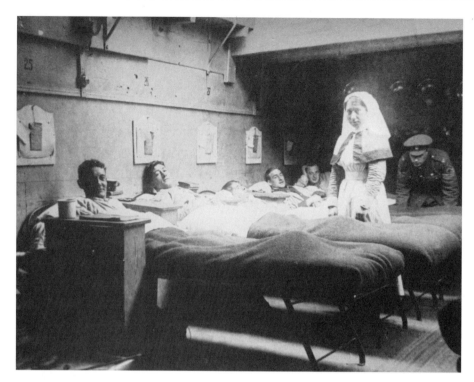

Care for the sick and wounded soldier had become a matter of social concern since the Crimea. Although conditions had improved greatly, the stark, barrack-like surroundings of a military hospital are clearly illustrated here. However the dedication of the nursing staff made up for the shortcomings in medical technology. (Private collection)

of tinned stew which was quite popular] or cheese and raw meat, [which would arrive] all mixed in the same sandbag. I never once had eggs or fresh fruit. Once I got a loaf that was all bloody, but we scraped the worst off and ate it. We were treated like beasts, and I never thought it was fair.'

The issue of a rum ration was a saving grace, especially in the winter months. At breakfast time an NCO with a large earthenware jar marked 'SRD'[1] would carefully dole out a measure to each man. It was Navy rum, not diluted, and its strength caught many unawares, leaving them watery-eyed and coughing. After a freezing night men insisted that they could feel its warmth spreading out into their fingers and toes, and if they exaggerated the physical effect, then it was certainly worth its issue for boosting morale.

Also eagerly awaited were the parcels sent from home. Packed by mothers, wives, sweethearts or simply collected by local people and sent en masse, their contents were a welcome diversion from the basic food rations. Sometimes, though, the contents were not so useful.

John Dalton once received a parcel from a schoolgirl in his home town that consisted of 'three pairs of very small socks, boiled sweets, a crushed fruit cake, a bible, a tin of vermin powder and a tract exhorting the reader to give up alcohol.' For many men at the front, parcels provided a lifeline with home, with small comforts such as tobacco, underwear, books and a host of other small items improving the life of the recipients.

Soldiers were past masters at 'scrounging' and many a meal was supplemented by fruit from nearby orchards, vegetables from garden plots, and even fresh meat if a farmer was unlucky to have an ex-butcher amongst the men billeted with him. After a Scottish battalion had left a well-stocked farm near Arras, the farmer claimed for the loss of '32 chickens and one pig'.

Officially the CO determined that they had been lost through enemy action, and his men were not responsible. Roast pork was served in the officers' mess for three days afterwards. Incidents such as this occurred throughout the front lines.

---

[1] Service Rations Department. Some men believed 'seldom reaches destination' was more accurate.

RELAXATION AND LEAVE

Once out of the line, there were few places for soldiers to go. The most popular were the estaminets found in every village. A cross between a café and a pub, it was the focal point for most off-duty soldiers. Wine and beer were cheap, and 'oeufs et pommes frites' were usually available, especially in exchange for a few tins of bully beef or jam. French women were less inhibited than their British counterparts, and many fond liaisons were formed. Most of the larger towns had red light districts, but social taboos were not easily shaken off. Will Wells spoke for many when he recalled his attitude towards the 'pleasure parlours'.

'They were used by a certain sort – none of my friends would have dreamed of it, although we were curious. A lot of Australians and Canadians went there, but they had a different upbringing and of course they were paid more.' Money was always in short supply. The majority of men allocated most of their pay to wives or parents, which left little for having a good time. The mere fact of being out of danger and in convivial company was enough to cheer up the most dour soldier. A few weak French beers added to the moment, and evenings would be spent singing, telling tall tales and being cheeky to the young girls who always seemed to inhabit the estaminets and bars.

Home leave was a rare commodity, and once every 14 months was an average. Usually no warning was given, simply a 'chit' detailing 'seven days leave, starting immediately'. Soldiers would arrive home filthy, lousy and exhausted, but it was

British troops march through a newly liberated town in Flanders. The two central figures illustrate well the typical marching order of the late war period. Although of the same unit, it is interesting to note that the man on the left wears 1908 webbing, whilst the man on the right has the 1914 leather equipment. (Trustees of Royal Armouries)

worth it. Fred Wood spent five days sleeping, having the luxury of a hot bath whenever he felt like it, and reading. Others enjoyed a more hectic social life, frequently in local pubs. Married men preferred the comfort and companionship of their families, and most found leaving them to return to the front a terrible ordeal. As much as anything, the sudden removal from peace and safety to a life of death and destruction was hard to reconcile. George Wells, upon arriving back in France, commented that within two days of his return to the front line, he was embroiled in a savage and major battle.

'The life I had left behind was as remote to me as the moon, and I felt that the front was all I had ever known. Nothing else seemed real.'

This was an attitude that became more acute the longer a man served. The life of comparative safety that existed in England seemed totally unreal compared to front-line service. A soldier's friends, their shared daily experiences and constant exposure to death in a multitude of forms was the reality that mattered. It was almost impossible for a man to convey the reality of life at the front to family or friends, even if social

convention had permitted such frank discussions.

When Harry Wood was on leave and having a quiet drink in his local, a family friend came up and slapped him on the back, commenting, 'I suppose you've been having the time of your life, young fellow.' Harry said, 'What I wanted to do was tell him what it was like to watch a man sniped in the head die, or collect up the parts of someone caught by a shell. But it just wasn't done, so I drank up and walked out.'

It was a gulf that grew wider as the war progressed, and which never closed. As one veteran said, 'Either you had been at the front, or you hadn't. That was all there was to it.'

For the vast majority of soldiers who had never before been abroad there were a multitude of attractions in the larger French towns, where the oddities of French life proved a constant source of fascination. Cafés, patisseries, restaurants and souvenir shops soon exhausted carefully hoarded funds, and evenings saw groups of men in varying stages of intoxication weaving unsteadily back to outlying billets before their leave passes expired, leaving them open to a charge.

Although gambling was officially forbidden,

Religion was an important social factor, most men having been brought up with some form of belief. The army catered for the major denominations, with Catholic and Anglican clerics attached to most battalions. Out of the line, church parades were compulsory, but the minority religious groups were left pretty much to their own devices. Men who entered their religion as atheist to avoid church parades usually found themselves doing extra cookhouse fatigues instead.

In the shared dangers of the line, belief was a common bond, not a division as it so often became in peacetime. It was not uncommon for prayers to be heard during lulls in particularly heavy bombardments. Thousands of men took great comfort in the facilities provided at Christian centres such as Toc H in Poperinghe, or the numerous YMCA rest rooms. Quite often they were the only place that men could relax in a civilised manner, and read or write. Tea, chocolate and food was always available at modest prices, and the dehumanising effect of the trenches could temporarily be thrown off.

A Territorial private of the 5th Gloucesters: he wears a nine-pouch bandolier (five at the front and four at the rear) as issued to mounted troops. These bandoliers held 90 rounds, whereas the five-pouch ones issued to infantry held only 50. (Author's collection)

there wasn't a regiment that didn't have its resident clique of near-professional gamblers. One of the most popular games was 'Crown and Anchor', which, although discouraged, was seldom officially prohibited. Card games of all sorts were popular. Some of the Irish soldiers in particular gained a popular reputation for their willingness to bet on anything, and one particular tale tells of two men standing in the open during an intense artillery bombardment, betting on when a particular landmark would be hit. When a flying splinter badly injured one, his friend insisted on carrying him back to an aid post. Refusing congratulations for his bravery, he insisted: 'If I hadn't brought the old devil back I'd never have got the five bob he owes me!'

DISCIPLINE

There was a strong tradition of repressive discipline in the army of 1914. The Regular Army was used to dealing with tough men, often ex-labourers, unskilled and poorly educated. The men of the new armies were a different breed. Willing volunteers, they came from a wider social cross-section, and many were of officer material. They expected to be treated as civilised men, not cannon fodder, but few exceptions were made for them.

Even for the best behaved soldier, it was difficult to avoid some form of punishment, albeit for a trivial offence. During the retreat from Mons in 1914, it was declared a punishable offence to 'steal fruit from the trees of a friendly nation'.

Army regulations list 27 punishable offences, from War Treason down to False Answering. Most soldiers fell foul of the rules at some point. Pvt. Wood noted that 'thieving was common, and

The difficulties of extracting casualties from the battlefield are amply illustrated in this photograph of stretcher bearers at Passchendaele. In such conditions bearers worked in teams of eight, relieving each other at regular intervals, as exhaustion set in. The man nearest the camera is wearing shorts and sandbag-wrapped puttees in an attempt to reduce the amount of mud clinging to his legs. (Imperial War Museum)

if you had your cap or shirt pinched, well, you had to pinch another or get crimed for it.' Punishments meted out depended on a number of factors. If a regiment were in the line, then minor crimes tended to be treated with less severity, but the general conduct of a soldier, and the testimony of his officer or senior NCO would count for a great deal. Many good soldiers in the line had reputations as troublemakers out of it. Pvt. Marshall recalled a sergeant who was regularly reduced to the ranks after picking drunken fights with the detested 'Redcaps', the Military Police. Once in the line, his coolness and authority always earned him back his stripes.

Not all were so lucky. 337 men were shot during the war for offences ranging from cowardice to sleeping on duty. Less drastic was 'field punishment', which involved being tied to a gunwheel or T-shaped frame and having to remain on public view for a set number of hours each day, no matter what the weather conditions. Although not painful, it was certainly uncomfortable and humiliating. At least one group of Australians was seen cutting loose a British soldier and threatening his guard with bayonets and bloody retribution if he were found tied up again.

The experienced NCOs took into account the strain of warfare on their men, and exercised a paternal control over them. When, after two days without rest, 18-year-old Jimmy Hughes dozed off when on sentry, he was shaken awake by his company sergeant-major, who told him, 'If Jerry came over now he'd shoot you. That's nothing compared to what I'll do if I catch you asleep again.' He then gave Hughes a sip from a flask full of rum, leaving him very much awake. Not all were so lucky. During the retreat from Mons, two guardsmen, who had not slept for five days, were found asleep on sentry.

Both were court-martialled and shot.

The relationship between the men and their officers was crucial in forming efficient fighting units. Men tended to admire 'traditional' officers, who possessed all of the upper-class public school values of their genre. Not only should they be able to command, but they should also be gentlemen. Scorn was poured upon officers who were drunkards, profane or uncaring about their men. This attitude mellowed as the war progressed, when lack of suitable officer material saw large numbers of men being promoted from the ranks. Pvt. Dalton (himself a pre-war volunteer who became a captain) commented that 'by 1918, soldiers would accept orders from officers that the 1914 regular would have made mincemeat of.'

It is a great credit to the selection process that so many competent officers were produced during the war. Many other ranks developed strong bonds with them, often going to extreme lengths to assist an officer in trouble. Countless medals were awarded to soldiers who risked their lives to bring 'their' officer back when wounded, even at the cost of their own lives. When Pvt. Marshall's captain was left wounded in a shellhole, a member of his Vickers team, never noted for his love of authority, made three attempts to locate him, having to be forcibly restrained when about to try a fourth time. Commanders realised the value of good officers, and any who showed a lack of fibre soon found themselves returned to depot or assigned to menial duties.

There were many other ways in which men could incur the wrath of the army. Contracting venereal disease was classified as a 'SIW' (self-inflicted wound), exactly the same as for a man who had shot himself. Soldiers convicted of such acts could be put in prison, though some were given the option of returning to the front line, with additional fatigues when out of it, army reasoning being that they should not be spared the dangers that their comrades were facing. Some men simply fell foul of bullying NCOs and although no ex-soldiers would openly admit to participation, there are several tales of unpopular NCOs being fatally shot or simply disappearing in action in strange circumstances. Authority was no guarantee of safety. Persistent offenders would be

Despite the heat of European summers, no special hot-weather clothing was issued. These two Royal Engineers wear both examples of tropical service tunics and issue shorts. The man on the right has a gold wound stripe underneath his service chevron. The practice of wearing shorts had originated in India before the war. (Richard Dunning)

sent to military prison – the 'glasshouse'. Renowned for their brutal discipline, the prisons took most of the toughest cases, overseen by the universally detested and feared Military Police .

As far as most men were concerned, the 'Redcaps' existed solely to make life for the average soldier as miserable as possible. Their powers were far reaching, from being able to shoot a man found behind the lines during an attack, to putting a man on a charge for having a tunic button unfastened. The sterling work that they did in keeping clogged roads open, and directing traffic under intense shellfire was largely ignored by the rank and file, who regarded them as an unmitigated nuisance. One ex-soldier recounted the attitude of the men towards the MP:

'A few were alright – they'd stick their heads into an estaminet and say, "We'll be coming back in ten minutes," which gave us a chance to leave, but others would burst in and lay about us with truncheons, no warning, nothing. We never trusted them, most were blokes who were no good for front line service, and a lot were bullies. When we were drinking with the Aussies it was different, though. I saw Aussies beat a group of Redcaps so badly that they were stretcher cases. They never bothered us if we had them with us.'

COMBAT AND TACTICS

The tactics of the Great War were based on experience of colonial wars of the late-19th century, and the general feeling amongst the general staff that any European war would be short and sharp. The trench system that developed was anathema to the High Command, who tried the most obvious methods of overcoming it. In practical terms, this meant extended artillery bombardment, to destroy wire and emplacements, which it conspicuously failed to do. By the time the attacking force had left their trenches the opposing lines were bristling with rifles and machine-guns. Advancing British soldiers were forbidden to fire at the enemy, but were required to hold their rifles at the port (across their chests), and tackle the enemy with grenades and bayonets. These tactics failed again and again, and many units adopted more flexible methods of attack to try to reduce casualties. It was not until 1917 that tactical doctrine began to change, with creeping barrages that moved with the infantry, tank support to deal with strongpoints, and fire and movement tactics within infantry platoons to enable them to get forward in the attack.

Despite the dangers, there was a familiarity about trench life that afforded the ordinary soldier a degree of comforting routine. All of this vanished once it became common knowledge that a 'big show' was in the offing. The illusion of security was soon shattered with the prospect of going 'over the top' as most experienced soldiers

Men of the 3rd Battalion the Worcestershire Regiment, 25th Division, hold a position on the Aisne, May 1918. The man at centre has 'souvenired' a revolver and field-glasses from an officer casualty. (Imperial War Museum)

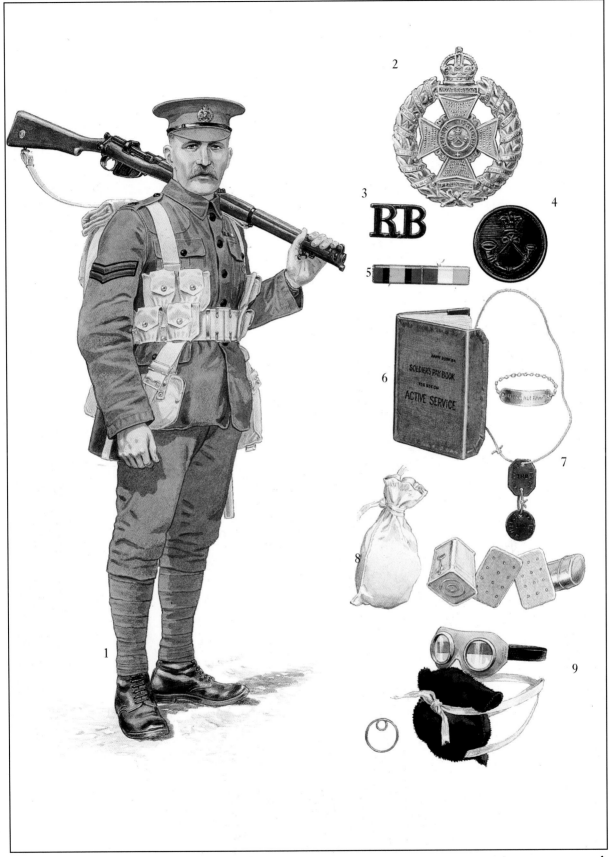

Corporal, Rifle Brigade, 1914 *(See text commentary for detailed captions)*

A

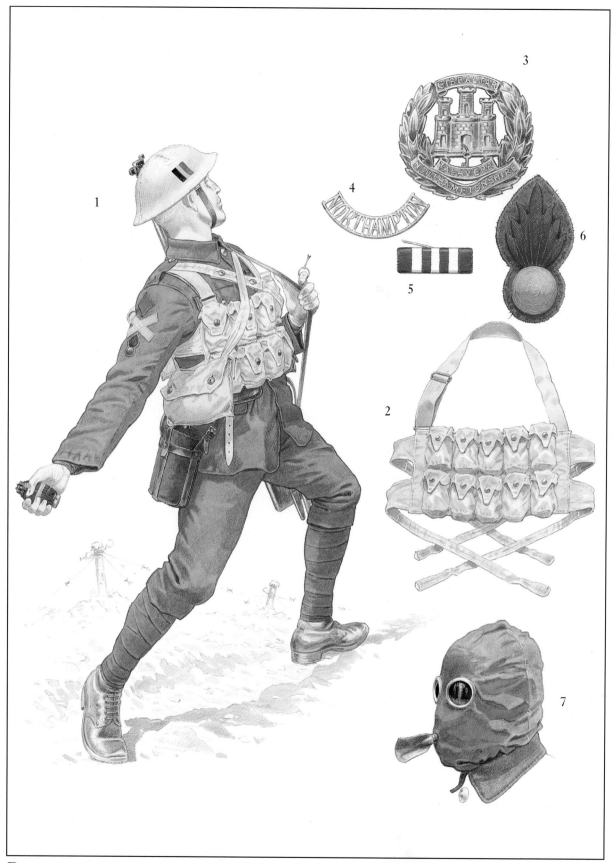

B

Private, 7th Northants, 1916 *(See text commentary for detailed captions)*

Infantry Lewis Gunner, 1917 *(See text commentary for detailed captions)*

C

D

Seaforth, Highlanders, 1918 *(See text commentary for detailed captions)*

Recruits for the 'New Armies' training in England, 1914–15

E

F

Royal Field Artillery, 1918

Vickers machine-gun detachment, 1918

G

H

Roadside scene, 1918

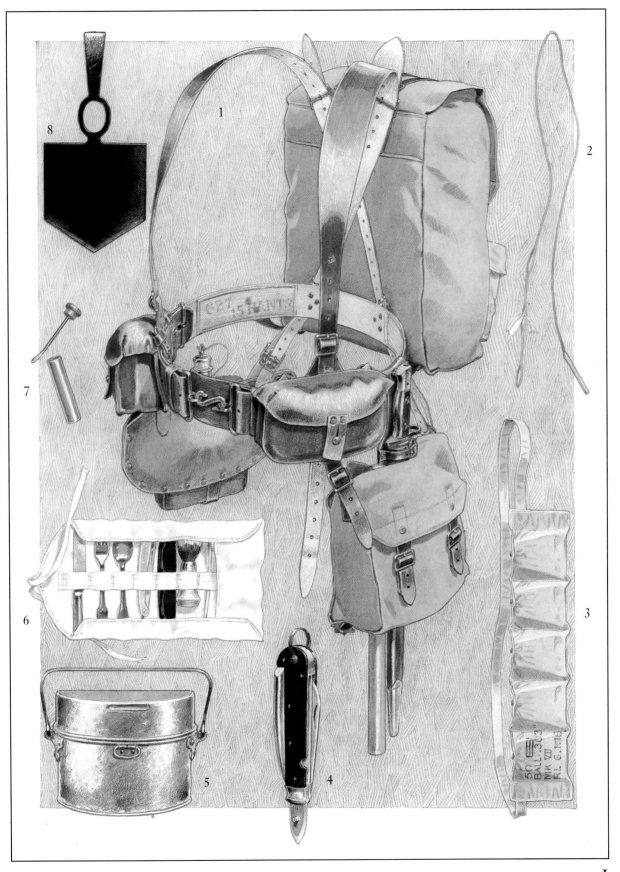

British Infantry equipment 1914–18 (*See text commentary for detailed captions*)

I

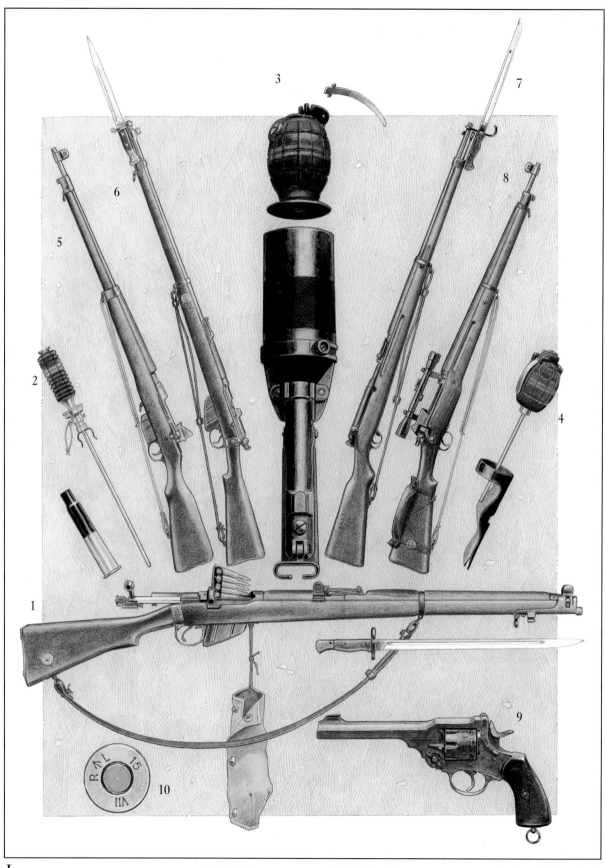

J   British Infantry weapons 1914–18 *(See text commentary for detailed captions)*

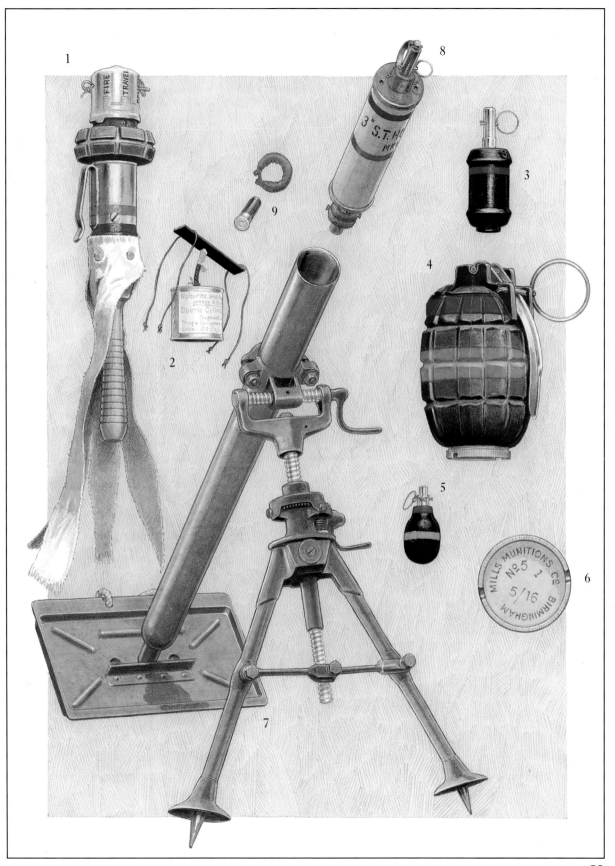

Grenades and the 3in. 'Stokes' light mortar *(See text commentary for detailed captions)*

K

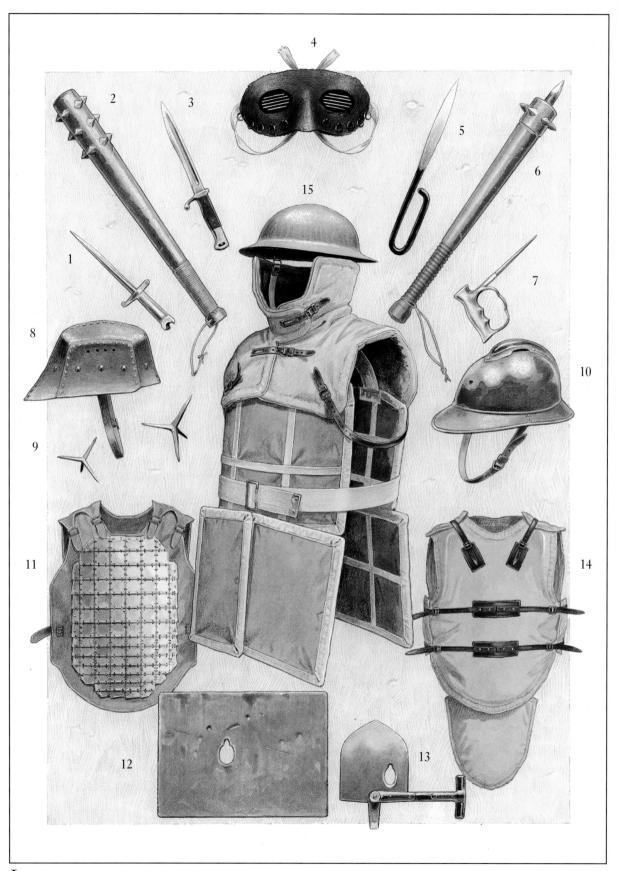

L Armour, clubs and daggers *(See text commentary for detailed captions)*

CAMBRAI

A dismounted tank crew, with Lewis guns. Each man wears 1914 leather equipment, with an open-topped revolver holster. Their box respirators are worn at the alert and several have leather and chain-mail 'splash masks' hanging on their belts. The officer, seated left, wears an officer's tunic with open collar, and a collar and tie. He also appears to be wearing a pair of whip cord breeches. (Author's collection)

knew how slim their chances of survival could be. Probably the worst affected were those who had never before experienced battle, as their imaginations ran riot with the terrors of the unknown that lay ahead of them. It was the waiting beforehand that was the hardest thing to come to terms with, and it affected men in different ways. Some became quiet and withdrawn, others cracked jokes to cheer their chums up. A few had premonitions about their futures, taking a friend into confidence.

Having been told his battalion of the Manchester Regiment, would be attacking the following morning, 19-year-old Pvt. Wells could not sleep. 'I crawled out of my dugout and stood staring at the stars, thinking I may never see them again. We had a man in our company called Charlie, who I had become very friendly with. He'd been over since Loos, and was very experienced. Well, he came up to me and stood puffing on his pipe. He asked me if I was frightened, and I said yes. He told me about his first battle, and how he never once fired his rifle,

and by the time he finished I was feeling better. He then said an odd thing, that he was sorry he hadn't got to know me earlier and it was a pity it was too late. Then he shook my hand and went.'

At the appointed hour, officers would blow their whistles, and the men would file quietly forwards, using scaling ladders to negotiate the steep parapet, usually into a hurricane of retaliatory small arms fire. Progress was slow, as the men were heavily laden: Pvt. Jarman carried 250 rounds of ammunition, Mills bombs in a bandoleer, and a shovel, as well as webbing, rifle and bayonet. Once they were clear of the trench, the men theoretically would hold formation around their officers, and keep extended line, whilst walking steadily towards the enemy.

A working party gets down to the job in hand. In the foreground a coil of wire is looped around steel crossbars, whilst screw pickets have been inserted ready for the wire to be threaded through. In the background a group of men are laying hardcore, possibly for a duckboard track. Apart from their steel helmets, there is little in their dress to indicate that this is a military unit.
(Trustees of Royal Armouries)

In practice, no man's land was an inferno of noise and smoke, with machine-gun bullets, shellfire and screams. Few men could concentrate on the task in hand, and Will Wells's experience was to remain with him for the rest of his life.

'We got into no man's land, and I followed the first line into the smoke. Everything seemed unreal – the noise was so great that it just became a constant sound, and I could see men dropping, like puppets with no strings. I wondered why they didn't keep up. I didn't recognise it then as a sign they had been shot dead. I kept close to old Charlie, and soon we were up to the wire. We were told not to bunch up, but men did which made them easier targets. A group of men were

running along, trying to find a way through the wire, and just folded up as a machine-gun caught them. Charlie jumped into a shellhole and I followed. When the fire slackened I asked him if we should go back, but he was dead, hit in the head by a bullet. At dusk I crawled back to our lines. It all seemed like a bad dream, but I didn't realise until next day how close I had been to dying.'

Not all attacks were such dismal failures. Even the General Staff learned eventually that frontal assaults on heavily defended positions were doomed to failure, and by 1917 a more flexible approach was being taken to fighting. For the battle of Messines, soldiers were taken to see scale models of the areas to be attacked, as well as being briefed on tactics and objectives. This was a far cry from previous years, and was appreciated by many rank and file. Harry Wood, by then a corporal, was impressed by the planning, and more so by the execution of it.

'Before zero hour, we crawled into dead ground in front of our trenches and lay there. When the

A motorised machine-gun unit, photographed some distance behind the lines: their uniform is a curious mixture of cavalry and infantry, with cavalry breeches and leather leggings. All the men wear 1908 pattern webbing pistol order: of particular note are the special 1908 'braces' attachments. Several men have removed the stiffening from their caps to give them a more battered appearance. (Author's collection)

barrage started, we got up and were in the trenches before Jerry knew what was happening. Most were too dazed by the mines to put up a fight. We left our mopping-up party behind and followed the barrage over the next [trench] and took their second line with little trouble. I had the Lewis gun and got great satisfaction from shutting up a German machine-gun post that had been bothering our flank. My officer told me that I'd get an award for it, but he was killed later, and I never did.

'The worst bit was holding the trench and waiting for reinforcements. Jerry tried counter-attacking, but we beat them off. They got so close that I had to use my pistol when the Lewis was empty. I wasn't frightened at all then, but got a bit shaky when we were relieved. I was glad to come out alive.'

Generally, men were too keyed up after battle to feel much except relief at their own survival. It was only after they were sent back to reserve lines or billets that their experiences began to prey on their minds. The loss of friends was particularly hard to bear, and small groups of silent men would be found wandering listlessly around.

'After roll call, I went around to see if any men I knew had come out (alive). There were almost no faces I recognised. I was really fed up and sat on my own. It seemed that the spirit of the battalion had gone with all the old faces, and I didn't think it would ever be the same. Six months later though, I was one of the "old sweats", and I realised that you can't dwell on the past, you just keep going.' (W. Wells)

The lucky ones were those able to walk out after combat. For the others, it was a different story.

CASUALTIES

Britain began the war with a small but relatively well-equipped medical service, and the system of aid posts, dressing stations, field hospitals and base hospitals served the army quite well at the outset. However, as the size of field armies increased, so did the numbers involved in battles, and the campaigns of 1915 such as Neuve Chapelle and Loos saw numbers of wounded arriving at the aid stations far beyond those contemplated in 1914.

The system of dealing with casualties relied on a network of treatment centres – Regimental Aid Posts behind the reserve trenches, casualty

A Hotchkiss gun section of the Suffolk Hussars: arguably a better designed weapon than the Lewis, it was clip-fed with a cyclic rate of 600 rpm. Several of the men carry Webley revolvers, and have special ammunition pouches to accommodate the Hotchkiss's hinged cartridge clips. (Author's collection)

clearing stations behind them, field hospitals and base hospitals behind those.

The medical services had considerable experience of dealing with high-velocity gunshot wounds, based on earlier colonial campaigns. For the ordinary soldiers, exposure to the effects of such injuries was unsettling to say the least. Many men wrote home about the effects of 'explosive bullets' fired by the Germans: in fact the energy contained within a standard .303in. or 7.92mm bullet was awesome. At close range (200–300m) such a projectile would punch clean through a man's torso with little loss of power, creating exit wounds that were several inches across. Men hit in the head rarely survived, regardless of the range, as shock caused massive internal damage. Even slight wounds could be complex, as bullets often travelled along bones. One man struck in the right wrist by a bullet had it travel up his arm, deflect off his collarbone, and exit from the top of the opposite shoulder. Wounds from shells were invariably worse, with razor-sharp, jagged chunks of steel flying hundreds of yards, and lead

shrapnel balls peppering the ground like giant shotgun blasts.

Lightly wounded men were expected to make their own way to aid posts, whilst the more serious cases waited to be collected by the stretcher bearers, who did heroic work in trying to reach the wounded, despite being frustrated both by enemy fire and the sheer numbers involved. In the first 24 days of the Somme battle, 136,000 men became casualties, 59,000 on the first day alone, overwhelming the medical service. Clarrie Jarman was one of them:

'We went over the top at Carnoy ... I had a bad gunshot wound in my right leg and was lucky to fall into a deep shellhole. The ground was covered with lads in khaki, dead, dying and wounded, and was being spattered with shrapnel, high explosive and bullets. I lay where I had fallen all day – about 14 hours. Again, I was lucky as a lad from the RAMC happened to come my way looking for wounded ... with the aid of a comrade they carried me back to the front line. After several hours I was placed on a stretcher and carried into the field dressing station, where my leg was dressed. Then I was sent to Amiens, but there were no beds, so I spent five days on the stretcher. I then went on a barge down the Somme River to Abbeville, where we got clean clothes before going by train to Boulogne. The hospital ships were full. At 3am on the 11th I arrived at Aberdeen.' By that time Clarrie's leg had been infected by gangrene and had to be amputated.

For an army that lived in the open, there were comparatively few minor ailments, such as colds. Fred Dixon commented that 'considering we were mainly volunteers, and not hardened to an outdoor life, we were all very healthy. If you got a cold it was gone in a couple of days.' More problematic were illnesses such as trench foot, cuts which invariably turned septic because of infection, and sheer exhaustion from lack of sleep.

Poor diet also resulted in boils and constipation, which was also, curiously, a common side effect of being under shellfire for any period of time. A form of trench fever also manifested itself sometimes, with flu-like symptoms. Most of these ailments were treated with a few days in a field

Casualties await their turn at a dressing station. During major offensives, thousands would be packed into fields and tents, whilst overworked doctors tried to deal with the most serious cases. Many men regarded any form of 'Blighty' (a popular name for 'England') wound as a godsend. (Courtesy Trustees of Royal Armouries)

hospital followed by 'light duty' for a week or so. Bad stomach problems were common, generally caused by drinking polluted water from shellholes. Water was always in short supply, and any source was welcome, the general assumption being that if boiled it would be alright. Pvt. Wells, living in a trench near Delville Wood, wrote: 'all things considered I am fine. We have been taking our water from a shellhole behind, and were surprised to find that the boot sticking out of it was still attached to a German. We are using a new hole now, but I don't suppose it makes much difference.' The problem of 'trench foot' was a serious one, being a form of gangrene brought about by having constantly wet feet exacerbated by poor circulation. It was actually considered a crime to contract it, and an afflicted soldier could be punished. Various remedies were tried, including issuing whale oil, which was to be rubbed into the feet on a daily basis. The best

Two soldiers get some rest in a typical 'funk hole'. These hastily excavated dugouts provided the minimum of protection from weather and shrapnel. The men have wrapped themselves in groundsheets. Note how the Enfield rifles to the right have issue canvas covers over their actions: both are also fitted with 1907 sword bayonets. (Imperial War Museum)

solution was dry footwear, and removal of boots and puttees whenever possible, to relieve pressure on swollen feet and legs. In mud-clogged trenches, this was easier said than done, as Pvt. Wells recalled:

'In Ypres, I never took my boots off for two weeks. When we came out of the line I had to cut my laces with a clasp knife, and when I got them [the boots] off the socks had rotted and my toes were black. I reported sick but I never lost any toes because the nurses were so good.'

The problem eased with the more widespread issue of waders, and more stringent checks by medical officers, but was never entirely eradicated.

Another persistent problem was that of venereal disease, and medical officers could do little to prevent wholesale infection. Affected men were sent back to base hospital for treatment but even placing notorious red-light areas out of bounds could not stop the problem. On average 800 men a month were admitted to hospital with one or other form of the disease. Lectures on hygiene were given noting simple precautions that could be taken to reduce risk, most of which were met

with a barrage of ribald comments, to the discomfort of the lecturer, and amusement of the men.

A problem that the army took some time to come to terms with was shellshock. In the early days of the war victims were treated as cowards, and many were severely punished, even to the extent of being executed. However, as the frontiers of medical knowledge moved forwards, so did the acceptance that exposure to severe concussion did cause mental instability ranging from headaches and shaking to complete mental breakdown. Treating such cases was another matter, with therapy ranging from electric shocks to cold baths. Then, as now, recuperation tended to be very much dependent on the individual, with some men making a total recovery whilst others never did. George Wells was badly shellshocked and remained affected all his life, flinching uncontrollably at loud noises and suffering poor hearing and stuttering.

There was little that could be done for the dead except to give them a decent burial where time and circumstances permitted. Most regiments tried to ensure this was done where possible, and bodies were wrapped in groundsheets or blankets, then placed behind the parados[2] to await removal to one of the small cemeteries that sprang up behind the lines. Burials were often attended by the dead man's comrades and presided over by the padre. Personal effects were gathered to be returned home, but useful items were usually shared out amongst friends. After Pvt. Dawson was killed, his friend, Pvt. Setchell, wrote a letter of condolence to the bereaved mother starting off: 'I am sorry about what happened as I was his friend. I have got his pocket knife'!

Thousands lay where they fell, to be buried later, or were hastily placed in shallow graves marked with a rifle and steel helmet, their sites lost in later fighting. Many were simply never found. Buried in dugouts, or vaporised by high explosive, they merely became names added to the growing list of 'missing presumed killed'. The many monuments to the missing which dot the countryside in France and Flanders are mute testament to them.

The Webley Fosbery self-cocking revolver: based on the issue Webley pistol, this ingenious design used the recoil from the cartridge to recock the action, by sliding the whole barrel and cylinder assembly to the rear. Although well made, it was too expensive and the mechanism too easily jammed for it to prove successful in trench warfare. (Courtesy Trustees of Royal Armouries)

ON CAMPAIGN

There was a depressing similarity in the conduct of most of the major battles of the Great War. From the onset of trench warfare in 1915 to the final breakthrough in 1918, gains were measured in hundreds of yards and tens of thousands of casualties.

Although the battles of the Somme, which began in July 1916, are often taken as typical of combat on the Western Front, they were significant only for the huge numbers of casualties and the amount of ordnance that they absorbed.

Arguably one could say the most important campaign was Cambrai, for although it did not achieve any lasting gain in terms of territory, it proved that there was a viable alternative to the endless and futile blood letting of trench warfare.

The planning and operation of the Cambrai battle was witnessed by two brothers, George and William Wells, one in the RAMC, the other in the Manchesters, who between them left behind an interesting record of the battle from the ordinary soldier's viewpoint.

The tactics of Cambrai were dictated by the staff of the Tank Corps, who had been begging for a chance to prove what tanks were capable of, given the right ground and sound planning. The concept of the battle was simple – a lightning attack along an extended front by tanks, with a creeping artillery barrage and the infantry in close support. There was to be no preliminary bombardment, always a giveaway of a forthcoming attack. The infantry involved included Pvt. William Wells, who had already survived the slaughter of Passchendaele. Planning for Cambrai was, to him, something of a revelation.

'We knew that something big was up, as we had been withdrawn from the line and put into reserve. One day we were told by our officer that we were going to take part in a surprise attack. This was a revelation, I can tell you. We had never known anything about our objectives before, other than the place we climbed out of the trenches. We saw a big scale model of the line, and were told how the tanks would go in first. A lot of us were able to look into the tanks

---

[2] The rear wall of the trench.

The pattern 1914 rifle was based on the Mauser action, and originally chambered for a .276in. (7mm) cartridge, an extremely powerful round. The demands of war in 1914 highlighted the difficulties of mass producing the SMLE. The P14 was easier and cheaper to make and was rapidly converted to .303in. Fitted with a telescopic sight, it made an excellent sniping rifle. (Trustees of Royal Armouries)

The Mk I .455in. Webley semi-automatic pistol: the only one of its type officially adopted by British forces, it was well designed although awkward to use. It was issued in considerable numbers to the Royal Navy, and in lesser quantities to the Royal Flying Corps. Some were privately purchased, and carried by infantry officers. (Trustees of Royal Armouries)

afterwards, and some of our officers had rides in them, which not many appreciated.'

A major factor in the planning of the battle was that of surprise. There was to be no preliminary barrage, and 378 combat tanks would advance on a six-mile front, working in groups of three and each carrying a fascine to fill the German trench, which was too wide to permit a tank to cross unaided. The infantry were to advance close behind, and as the tanks worked up and down the enemy lines they would rush the defenders with little opposition. Will Wells was naturally sceptical, having experienced the opposition from the Germans at Ypres despite being assured that the artillery would have destroyed the enemy trenches. 'I knew that Jerry was a tough fighter, and most of us reckoned it would be another Ypres. We didn't reckon much to the chances of the tanks.' On the night of 19 November 1917, he and his comrades were marched up to the front line near Flesquières, and issued with extra ammunition. He had been appointed runner, with instructions to stay close to his company commander. He promptly ditched most of his ammunition and grenades. 'If I was a runner, I reckoned the last thing I wanted was to carry an extra 10lb of ammo.' They then settled down to wait for dawn.

In a front line aid post, George Wells had spent hours checking and double checking his medical supplies, stacking dozens of stretchers and hundreds of dressings. Having served since 1915, he was under no illusions what the following day would bring. 'When there was a big battle on, we simply couldn't stop to rest. I was used to being on my feet for two days without a break. I was used to the awful sights by then, and could tell quite quickly who was worth saving and who was not.'

At dawn on 20 November, the tanks started

into no man's land as a deluge of shells crashed onto the German lines. As they lurched off into the early mist, the infantry rose stiffly, slightly fortified by an early issue of rum, and clambered over the parapet. For Pvt. Wells, it proved an unusual experience.

'There was no retaliation from Jerry, and I kept thinking, "any minute, those guns will open up" but they didn't. They [the tanks] had simply crushed the wire flat. We just walked over it like it wasn't there, with almost no opposition.'

The first wave of British troops swept over the German front line, meeting only dazed German soldiers who soon surrendered. The British artillery barrage continued to move ahead of the advancing troops, forcing the defenders into cover until their attackers were on top of them. Opposition began to stiffen as return shellfire found targets with the crawling tanks, and German machine-gun crews braved the shells to set up their guns. Pvt. Wells found himself and his officer pinned down in the German second line. 'We had lost contact with our company. I think a lot were still in the front trench. My officer pulled out a pad and scribbled a message, saying to me, "Give this to the first tank you can find," and off I went. It was quite clear by then, and I could see where the tanks were from the shells bursting around them. I got near one and realised it was burning so I made for another. I used my rifle butt to bang on the door and attract their attention. When a crewman stuck his head out I gave him the note, and ran back to the trench. I thought being near tanks was too unhealthy. When I got back my company had moved on, so I joined with another.'

Meanwhile the battle moved ahead with incredible speed. In the space of 24 hours a salient five miles deep had been driven into the German lines across a seven-mile front. Initial casualties (1,500 men) were about one three-hundredth of what would normally have been expected for such

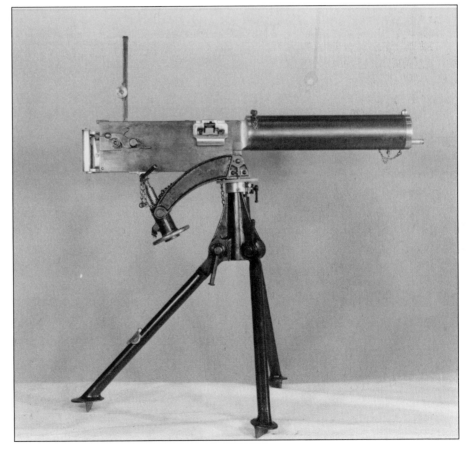

An early .303in. Vickers-Maxim: its brass and gun-metal body was too expensive for wartime production, and it was replaced in 1915 by the lighter and cheaper Vickers Mk I. Throughout the war, Germany continued to use an almost identical variant of the Vickers-Maxim. (Courtesy Trustees of Royal Armouries)

Somme, March 1918: weary Tommies make good use of a pram to bring in a stretcher case. They are wearing the sleeveless leather jerkin, introduced in 1916. (Imperial War Museum)

gains. For George Wells in the aid post it was a puzzling time. 'Casualties started trickling back, but only in small numbers. They kept telling us how Jerry had upped sticks and left his trenches, but I didn't believe them. We kept saying that any moment the real works would begin, but it didn't.'

Unbeknown to him, his brother was in the thick of the fighting. Having pushed beyond the trenches into open country, his battalion was running short of ammunition and had dug in overnight. Meanwhile German retaliation had begun.

'We could see a big wood away to our front, and the Jerries could see us. A couple of times one of their aircraft flew low over us, firing its machine-guns. Then their artillery started up. We couldn't do much about it, but a while later it stopped suddenly, and we saw a mass of troops heading towards us. We let fly, and our Lewis guns stopped them, but after a bit we were told they were flanking us, so we started to fall back. On both sides of me, my chums were hit but we couldn't stop. One kept trying to crawl after us, and eventually I lost sight of him.'

The success of the battle was to be short-lived, however. General Byng had insufficient reserves to support the advance, and German counter-attacks soon pushed the British line back. At the end of the day casualties and prisoners on each side were about equal, and no permanent gains had been made.

By then calls for stretcher bearers ensured George Wells was fully occupied in the front line and beyond, collecting wounded, but it was to be his last battle.

'On the second day we had an officer from the Tanks in, who was very worried about his crew, who he had left near their vehicle. He was badly wounded in the arm and hip, but insisted we went back with him to find them. Four of us followed him, and after some trouble found two of them in a shellhole. The tank was just twisted metal. I don't know how they survived, but we gave them morphine and dressed their wounds. As we were heading back I saw a flash, and then something blew me off my feet. That was the last I knew till I came to in base hospital.'

Having survived a near direct hit from an artillery shell, Pvt. Wells suffered from bad shellshock, which resulted in his being invalided out of the army in 1918.

If not an unqualified success, Cambrai paved the way for a more flexible form of warfare, doing away with wasteful preliminary bombardments (which mainly served to warn of impending attack) and relying on increased use of armoured units working in close co-operation with infantry and artillery.

The problem of supply had been addressed by the novel use of 98 supply tanks, hauling sledges full of ammunition, water and supplies, saving thousands of infantry man-hours. More importantly, it proved that the two greatest stumbling blocks – wire and trenches – could be overcome.

VISITING THE BATTLEFIELD

In the last decade, there has been a dramatic increase in visitors to the battlefields of the Great War. There are now a number of firms specialising in visiting the Western Front, but for the visitor who prefers to wander at a more leisurely pace there are a number of places of specific interest which are worth visiting. The best way to do this is to equip yourself with one of the battlefield guides available, some of which are listed below.

Please remember the battlefields are mainly private property, and whilst the farmers are incredibly tolerant, it is polite to avoid fields with crops or livestock in them. There are also huge quantities of live ammunition still in the ground. Leave well alone, for after 70 years it is dangerously unstable.

Guides

J. Giles, *The Somme Then and Now*
Ypres Then and Now
The Western Front Then and Now
R. Coombes, *Before Endeavours Fade*
V. Neuberg, *A Guide to the Battlefields of the Great War*
M. Middlebrook, *The Somme Battlefields – A Comprehensive Guide*

PLATES

A: Corporal, Rifle Brigade, 1914
1: The NCO depicted is a typical 'Old Contemptible' regular of the original B.E.F. serving with the 1st Battalion of his regiment in the 11th Infantry Brigade, 4th Division. He wears the 1908 pattern infantry equipment 'marching order' which contains 150 rounds of .303in. rifle ammunition, water bottle, entrenching tool, bayonet, greatcoat, ground sheet, mess tin and rations, as well as personal items, etc. He carries a Short Magazine Lee-Enfield rifle Mk III. Note his regimental-pattern chevrons and the insignia shown in detail on the right.

These include 2: the cap badge, 3: shoulder title and 4: black button of the Rifle Brigade, and 5: the ribbons of the 1899–1902 'Boer War'. Soldiers of the B.E.F. carried a record and pay book containing personal details (6), and wore identity discs (official) and bracelets (unofficial) as shown (7). 8: Field rations issued were carried in a ration bag and included 'bully beef' and hard biscuits. An emergency 'iron ration' was carried in an oval sectioned tin. With the advent of the first gas attacks in 1915 the first primitive gas masks were issued (9) which included goggles, cotton waste pads in a gauze holder, and a nose clip.

B: Private, 7th Northants, 1916
1: A 'bomber' serving with a 'Kitchener' battalion, the 7th Battalion the Northamptonshire Regiment, the subject wears the 1914 pattern infantry

Lance Corporal Jim Marshall, Machine-gun Corps: an interesting picture for the amount of insignia shown. On his left sleeve is visible a single gold wound stripe, above which is a good conduct chevron, topped with a brass-wreathed MG badge, showing him to be a qualified gunner. On his shoulder over the NCO's stripe is a cloth cross, possibly a brigade insignia. His brass shoulder titles 'I MGC' indicate Machine-gun Corps Infantry. (Author's collection)

equipment in its 'fighting' order and 2: a 10-pocket 'waistcoat' carrier for grenades, in this case the No. 5 'Mills'. Even without the pack and its contents, the additional weight of steel, two gas equipment haversacks and ten 1½lb grenades was considerable. Note the regimental colours stencilled on the helmet cover, the 'battle insignia' of the 24th Division indicating 73rd Infantry Brigade, 7th Northants, and 'A' Company. Below these is the badge of a 'bomber', a red flamed grenade. On his left breast is the ribbon of the Military Medal, introduced in 1916 to reward acts of bravery. Details to the right include (from top to bottom) 3: the wartime, all brass version of the Northants cap badge, 4: the regimental shoulder title, 5: the ribbon of the M.M. and 6: the 'bombers' badge. Below these are the grenade waistcoats and 7: the 'PH' Phenate Hexamine gas helmet.

C: Infantry Lewis Gunner, 1917
1: A private soldier of the 10th Battalion (1st Gwent) South Wales Borderers, 38th (Welsh) Division, a New Army formation. He carries and operates a Lewis gun, a .303in. gas-operated, air-cooled automatic weapon, not termed a machine-gun at the time. Fed by a radial magazine containing 47 rounds of ammunition, the Lewis had a cumbersome barrel casing surrounding a complicated system of aluminium barrel cooling fins. This brought the weight of the weapon, with a full magazine, to about 30lb, hardly a light weapon.

His equipment is the 1914 pattern leather infantry equipment, with the pouch and holster for the .455in. Smith and Wesson revolver and ammunition, helmet, 'small box' respirator, and at his feet, pouches and panniers for the Lewis's magazines. These would be carried by others in his section. Note the patch of the 10th S.W.B. on his helmet cover, the divisional sign of the 38th Division, the red dragon of Wales on his left sleeve, the battalion/brigade indicator on his right sleeve, the 'L.G.' skill-at-arms badge, good conduct chevron and two wound stripes.

Detail includes (top to bottom) 2: the cap badge of the South Wales Borderers, 3: their shoulder title, 4: the helmet patch of the 10th S.W.B., 5: the Lewis gun skill-at-arms badge, 6: the 10th S.W.B. battalion/brigade badge. Many patterns of revolver were issued to British troops from 1915 onwards. 7: shown here with its cleaning rod, .455in. rounds, pouch and Lanyard is the 'Pistol, O.P., No. 1 Mark I', a weapon purchased from Spain.

D: Seaforth Highlander, 1918
1: The figure depicted is a lance corporal, regimental signaller, of the 2nd Battalion, Seaforth Highlanders (Ross-shire Buffs, the Duke of Albany's), 10th Infantry Brigade, 4th Division, B.E.F., France, 1918. He wears the 1908 pattern webbing 'field service marching order' (F.S.M.O.)

which by then included a respirator, steel helmet and sundry other small items. Note the MacKenzie tartan of his kilt, bonnet and shoulder patches, the 'Seaforth' garters, and the chevrons of appointment, good conduct and overseas service. Three gold wound stripes, signaller's crossed flags and the green patch of the 10th Brigade. He sports a leather jerkin, a waterproof rifle cover, has his kilt apron and respirator atop his pack and has the green bar of his battalion painted on his helmet. 'Out since Mons', he has visible the insignia of the veteran.

Other detail includes (top to bottom) 2: the bonnet badge, and 3: shoulder title of the Seaforth Highlanders, 4: the 'ramshead' patch of the 10th Infantry Brigade, 5: overseas service stripes from 1914-18, 6: a wound stripe, 7: the ribbon of the 1914 Star (issued from late 1917), 8: the 1917 issue 'small box' respirator, 9: haversack, 10: nose clip, 11: filter box of the respirator, 12: tear gas

An unusual photograph illustrating one of the more dangerous trench pastimes, namely setting the fuses of Stokes mortar bombs. Although not as hazardous as fusing Mills grenades, it was still a risky business, and was usually undertaken by small groups separated by sandbagged walls, to minimise the damage in the event of an explosion. (Imperial War Museum)

goggles, 13: first field dressing, iodine ampoule and the shell dressing for large wounds.

E: Recruits for the 'New Armies' training in England, 1914–15

The 'Kitchener' men had to wait many months before proper uniforms and equipment became available. For weeks they drilled in their civilian clothes until the interim blue uniforms shown were issued. Our subjects wear the obsolete Slade-Wallace equipment and are armed with elderly Lee-Metford rifles, reissued for drill purposes. They are performing bayonet exercises under the supervision of a member of the Army Gymnastics Staff. The nearest soldier has parried the instructor's training stick and directs a 'Long Point!' to the throat of the bayonet dummy. To the rear a second man performs the 'Withdraw!'

The white patches on the sleeves of the recruits indicate the 19th Battalion, the King's (Liverpool Regiment), a service battalion with the 30th Division, raised by Lord Derby and known as the '3rd City' or 'Liverpool Pals'. A training stick lies in the foreground. Pupils were required to parry and dodge the padded end in order to thrust their bayonets through the ring on the other end.

F: Royal Field Artillery, 1918

Bringing up ammunition to a battery of 18-pdr field guns in action: the central figure is a driver, R.F.A., of the divisional artillery, 51st (Highland) Division, leading a horse which is carrying eight rounds of 18-pdr ammunition. These are in a pannier thrown across a standard 1912 pattern saddle. The animal's bridle is the standard 1902 pattern, with the horse's anti-gas respirator attached.

The driver wears the service dress of a mounted soldier, steel helmet and a 'small box' respirator. Note the badge of the Royal Artillery painted on his helmet beside the divisional sign of the 51st. The latter is repeated on his sleeves in the colours of the R.A. Note also his R.F.A. titles, good conduct chevron for two to five years' service, his two gold wound stripes, and the whips-and-spur badge for proficiency in driving. Our subject wears the ribbon of the Military Medal, a white lanyard, and the spurs of a mounted soldier. To the rear, mules are seen delivering ammunition to an 18-pdr gun. Note the crew working in shirt-sleeves, the dapp-camouflage paint scheme on the gun and the observing aircraft above.

G: Vickers machine-gun detachment, 206th M.G. Company, 58th (21st London) Division, T.F., 1918

This team is seen here firing at 2,500 yards in support of an attack visible on the horizon. All the equipment of a Vickers in action is visible including ammunition boxes, belts and cartridge

A splendid illustration of Pvt. A.F. Carter, 4th Middlesex Regiment, taken near Mons on 22 August 1914. He wears the 1908 pattern equipment to which has been added a modified 1903 haversack. His Mk I Lee-Enfield is fitted with the early pattern 1907 bayonet with its distinctive hooked quillon, ordered to be removed in 1913 from service bayonets to prevent snagging: many existing ones remained like this, though. Surprisingly, Pvt. Carter survived the war. (Courtesy The Mons Museum)

cases. The 'No.2' carries the spare-parts case and an oil bottle and cleaning/clearing rod is seen in the foreground. Both men are shown wearing 'small box' respirators and 'fighting order' 1908 pattern webbing equipment. Note the divisional sign of the 58th Division, a stylised Tower of London, painted on the helmets, the violet saltire of the 206th company on the jacket sleeves and – just visible – on the front of the helmet of the corporal 'No. 1'. 'MGC' over 'I' titles are worn on the shoulder straps, overseas service stripes, introduced in early 1918, are worn on the right cuff, and the corporal has the 'MG' skill-at-arms badge above his rank chevrons. The 'No.1' is armed with a .455in. revolver, and the 'No.2' with a SMLE rifle. The 58th Division played a major role in the fighting to reclaim the ground lost to the Germans in March–April 1918, and the plate depicts a typical action of the summer of 1918.

H: Roadside scene, 1918

A Mark IV *male* tank of the 7th Battalion, Tank Corps, has broken down on the bank of a sunken road. Two Tank Corps staff officers are using the elevated position of the tank to observe fighting going on in the distance. Infantry line the opposite bank whilst spotting aircraft are drawing 'Archie' fire. In the foreground a corporal of the 7th Tanks converses with a 'Don R' of the divisional signal company, Royal Engineers, 25th Division. Note the red-over-green colours on the shoulder strap and painted on the helmet of the corporal, the 'T.C.' titles stitched on the sleeves, the tank crew qualification badge, badges of rank and overseas service stripes. His equipment

includes an anti-splash visor, 'small box' respirator, 1914 pattern leather equipment and a .455in. revolver.

He wears 'canvas' overalls and carries the spanner for adjusting track tension. The machine of the despatch rider is a Model 'H' 1915 Triumph, a 550cc motorcycle capable of a top speed of 45mph. Note the vehicle divisional sign of the 25th Division, a red-and-white chequerboard device, over the colours of a signals unit. The latter is repeated on the brassards worn by the rider. Note the red horseshoe worn on the uniform by the men of the 25th Division, and the equipment of a 'Don R', which includes goggles, gauntlets, leggings, and a .455in. revolver in a 1914 pattern belt.

An 'al fresco' lunch: bottled beer and a box of sandwiches would seem to indicate a fairly quiet area of the front. The stone jar is one of the coveted issue 'SRD' rum jars, which once drained of their original contents proved far better for holding precious water than the usual petrol tins.
(Courtesy Trustees of the Royal Armouries)

Technology had made a big impact on the course of the war by 1918. This tank of the 1st Gun Carrier Company is being used as a supply vehicle at Villers-Brettonneaux in 1918. It could carry within its body and on a towed wooden sledge the same quantity of supplies and munitions that would have required nearly a battalion of infantrymen to transport earlier in the war. (Courtesy of the Tank Museum, Bovington)

I: British infantry equipment, 1914–18
1: This shows the 1914 pattern leather infantry equipment, assembled in its full 'marching' configuration with the pack buckled to the back and the haversack on the left side. Each pouch contained 50 rounds of ammunition in a cotton bandoleer, and the entrenching tool was carried beneath the water bottle on the right side with its handle strapped to the bayonet on the left side. The main item carried in the pack was the greatcoat, and the mess tin in a khaki cotton case was strapped to the outside.

Other items carried included: 2: a whipcord 'pull through' for cleaning the rifle's bore; 3: extra ammunition carried in a cotton bandoleer; 4: a jack-knife; 5: mess tin; 6: a 'holdall' for items such as cutlery, razor, comb, lather brush, toothbrush, etc. 7: Oil bottle (this and the 'pull through' were carried in the butt of the rifle; 8: Mattock-head of the entrenching tool.)

J: British infantry weapons, 1914–18
1: The main infantry weapon of the British army in the Great War was the Short Magazine Lee-Enfield rifle (SMLE), shown here with its bolt open, charger inserted, and with sling and breech cover attached. The 1907 pattern bayonet is beside it. 2: the No. 3 rifle grenade with grenade cartridge beside it; 3: the later No. 36 rifle grenade was fired from a discharge cup; and 4: the No. 23 rifle grenade from a sheet steel device attached to the rifle by means of the bayonet.

Many other patterns of rifle were acquired and pressed into service from 1914 onwards. These included 5: the Canadian Ross Mark III; 6: the obsolete Lee-Enfield; 7: the Japanese Arisaka Type 38; 8: and the American manufactured P-14 shown here with a 1918 pattern telescopic sight and improvised cheek pad.

There were many patterns of pistol in use from 1914 to 1918 also, as well as several patterns or 'marks' of the regulation .455in. Webley revolver. The most numerous of the Webleys was 9: the Mark VI. 10: base of a round for the Mark VII .303in. ammunition, the standard service rifle and machine-gun ammunition.

K: Grenades and the 3in. 'Stokes' light mortar

The British army went to war with 1: the No. 1 grenade, which had been designed in 1908 and was almost as dangerous to the thrower as to the enemy. The shorter handle of the Mark II made the grenade somewhat safer. Note the canvas streamers intended to ensure the grenade fell onto the percussion fuse. Demand for grenades led to designs as crude as 2: the No. 8, made from food tins and fired by a Brock match drawn across a 'brassard' igniter. By 1917 effective designs of grenade were in mass production, and these included 3: the No. 27 white phosphorous grenade for the production of smoke and dugout clearance, 4: the No. 5 'Mills' grenade and 5: the lighter No. 34 'egg' grenade. The 'Mills' was the first safe and effective grenade issued to British troops, but at 1½lb could not be thrown far, placing the British at a disadvantage when encountering the German 'egg' grenade. This was remedied with

For many men, the harsh reality of war was a profound shock after a childhood spent listening to tales of Victorian derring-do. Most men developed a strong sense of callousness as a form of protection against the sights they were exposed to, the memory of which later in post-war life could reduce them to tears. (Imperial War Museum)

the introduction of the 12oz No. 34 grenade, which was a copy of the German weapon. On munitions of this type a red band denoted an explosive filling, whilst the second band denoted the type. Green was for Amatol, and pink for Ammonal or Bellite. 6: Typical markings on the base plug of a No. 5 grenade can be seen here.

7: The 3in. 'Stokes' light mortar of 1915 looks remarkably similar to the designs of today. The barrel, base plate, and mounting (bipod) together weighed 113lb and launched a bomb (8) weighing 10¾lb. Propellent power was provided by the 12-bore cartridge (9) and augmenting ring charges at the base of the bomb. At its head is shown the service time fuse head. The maximum range of the mortar bomb with four rings was 710 yards.

L: Armour, clubs and daggers
1: Bayonet-dagger for Mk VI Webley revolver; 2: trench club; 3: dagger made from ground-down German bayonet; 4: tank mask (a chain mail curtain was attached to the rings); 5: ordnance-made dagger; 6: trench club; 7: push-dagger and knuckle-duster; 8: fibre helmet for tank crews; 9: Caltrops, scattered in no-man's land to spike the unwary; 10: French 'Adnan' helmet (a quantity of these were supplied to British formations before the 'Brodie' shrapnel helmet became available); 11: The 'Franco–British' cuirass of 1916 (plate armour); 12: loophole trench shield; 13: MacAdam shield/ shovel; 14: the 'E.O.B.' body armour of 1917, an officially issued armour; 15: British body armour of 1916, comprising 'Brodie' steel helmet, layered-silk 'necklet' and 'Drayfield' body shield.

FURTHER READING

There are so many published works covering the war that any selection must be subjective. To the best of the author's knowledge, all the personal narrative titles listed below are currently available, mostly as reprints of the originals.

General history

M. Middlebrook, *The First Day on the Somme*
A. Simpson, *Hot Blood and Cold Steel*
  The Evolution of Victory: British Battle on the Western Front
L. MacDonald, *The Roses of No Man's Land*
  1914
  1915
  The Somme
  They called it Passchendaele
  Voices of the Great War
M. Chappell, *The Somme 1916*

Personal narratives

A. Barrie, *War Underground – The Tunnelers of the Great War*
C. Carstairs, *A Generation Missing*
E. Campion Vaughan, *Some Desperate Glory*
G. Coppard, *With a Machine-gun to Cambrai*
C. Douie, *The Weary Road – Recollections of an Infantry Subaltern*
R. Graves, *Goodbye to All That*
E. Junger, *Storm of Steel*
F. Richards, *Old Soldiers Never Die*
S. Sassoon, *Memoirs of a Fox-Hunting Man*
J. Lucy, *There's a Devil in the Drum*

INDEX

References to illustrations are shown in **bold**.

COMPANION SERIES FROM OSPREY

MEN-AT-ARMS
An unrivalled source of information on the organisation, uniforms and equipment of the world's fighting men, past and present. The series covers hundreds of subjects spanning 5,000 years of history. Each 48-page book includes concise texts packed with specific information, some 40 photos, maps and diagrams, and eight colour plates of uniformed figures.

WARRIOR
Definitive analysis of the appearance, weapons, equipment, tactics, character and conditions of service of the individual fighting man throughout history. Each 64-page book includes full-colour uniform studies in close detail, and sectional artwork of the soldier's equipment.

ORDER OF BATTLE
The most detailed information ever published on the units which fought history's great battles. Each 96-page book contains comprehensive organisation diagrams supported by ultra-detailed colour maps. Each title also includes a large fold-out base map.

CAMPAIGN
Concise, authoritative accounts of history's decisive military encounters. Each 96-page book contains over 90 illustrations including maps, orders of battle, colour plates, and three-dimensional battle maps.

NEW VANGUARD
Comprehensive histories of the design, development and operational use of the world's armoured vehicles and artillery. Each 48-page book contains eight pages of full-colour artwork including a detailed cutaway.

AIRCRAFT OF THE ACES
Focuses exclusively on the elite pilots of major air campaigns, and includes unique interviews with surviving aces sourced specifically for each volume. Each 96-page volume contains up to 40 specially commissioned artworks, unit listings, new scale plans and the best archival photography available.

COMBAT AIRCRAFT
Technical information from the world's leading aviation writers on the century's most significant military aircraft. Each 96-page volume contains up to 40 specially commissioned artworks, unit listings, new scale plans and the best archival photography available.